Plan Your Kitchen
hundreds of design combinations at-a-glance

COLLINS | DESIGN
An Imprint of HarperCollins*Publishers*

Introduction by **Lorrie Mack**

PLAN YOUR KITCHEN: HUNDREDS OF AT-A-GLANCE DESIGN COMBINATIONS
Copyright © 2006 by Axis Publishing Ltd.

HarperCollins books may be purchased for educational, business, or sales promotional use.
For information, please write: Special Markets Department, HarperCollins Publishers,
10 East 53rd Street, New York, NY 10022.

First Edition

First published throughout the world in English in 2006 by:
Collins Design
An Imprint of HarperCollins*Publishers*
10 East 53rd Street, New York, NY 10022
Tel: (212) 207-7000, Fax: (212) 207-7654
collinsdesign@harpercollins.com
www.harpercollins.com

Distributed throughout the world by:
HarperCollins*Publishers*
10 East 53rd Street
New York, NY 10022
Fax: (212) 207-7654

Created and conceived by:
Axis Publishing Limited
8c Accommodation Road, London NW11 8ED, UK
www.axispublishing.co.uk

Creative Director: Siân Keogh
Editorial Director: Anne Yelland
Managing Editor: Conor Kilgallon
Designer: Sean Keogh
Production: Jo Ryan, Cécile Lerbière

ISBN-10: 0-06-089196-3
ISBN-13: 978-0-06-089196-1

Library of Congress Control Number: 2001012345

Printed and bound in China
1 2 3 4 5 6 7 /12 11 10 09 08 07 06
First printing, 2006

A note on measurements
The dimensions of appliances, sinks, faucets, and lights are given in the form:
H = height
W = width
D = depth
These are followed by measurements in inches to the nearest $1/8$ inch,
and (in parentheses) in millimeters.

contents

The preparation and sharing of food are key elements in almost all of our relationships—with family, friends, neighbors, and colleagues. The strong emotional link we have with food makes the kitchen the practical and psychological heart of every home, whether it's a bachelor apartment or a multiroom mansion. So investing time, care, and resources in the design of this special space is actually a form of nurturing—of ourselves, and of the people we care for.

Creating a kitchen you love is as much about basic knowledge and common sense as it is about large budgets and flights of fancy. First, it involves identifying those elements you should spend money on, and those you can replace with ingenuity and style. Never scrimp underfoot, for example: cheap tiles or sheet flooring will mark easily and wear quickly. But if you can't afford a new table, it won't matter if you settle for a second-hand one, and hide it under a wipe-clean cloth.

BELOW When your starting point is such a stunning architectural framework as this one—light, lofty spaces and sculptural stairs and columns—allow it to take center stage by keeping the color and detailing simple and classy.

It's also important to take a clear look at what you actually do in your kitchen. If you're a keen cook or you cater for a large family every day, you'll want capacious, high-tech appliances, lots of work space, more than one sink, and plenty of storage. If you seldom prepare a meal from scratch, however, and rarely feed more than two, you'll be much better off with simple, compact appliances, and you can make do with much less storage space.

Apart from the big basic pieces like refrigerator and range, invest only in equipment and appliances that suit your habits and preferences; if you don't eat much toast, or many sandwiches, for example, a bread maker will never earn its counter

ABOVE Spot the subtle, geometric theme in this workmanlike space: the floor and wall tiles, the spice drawers on the top right, and the glazed panels in the cabinets are all perfect squares. Graceful period chairs and folksy floral plates prevent the theme from becoming an obsession.

ABOVE If you like to have all of your favorite things on hand and on permanent display, look for extra-deep cabinets and countertops. For a neat finish, create a shallow splashboard from the same material as your countertop.

LEFT The antithesis of a kitchen that looks like a hospital operating room, this extravagant decorating scheme features art nouveau light fittings together with tapestry pillows.

space. Even a set of designer saucepans or some mixing bowls will get in the way if you find that you hardly ever use them.

Once the practicalities are out of the way, you are free to enjoy one of the most personal and fulfilling elements of planning a room—choosing a decorating scheme. Remember that by their nature, kitchens are full of working clutter, so never add more in the form of busily patterned wallpaper or textiles, or stenciled motifs. Especially in small spaces, but often in big ones too, a good plan is to pick a shade you love, and use it for walls, cabinets, woodwork, and even flooring. This way, you'll create a cohesive sweep of background color that complements the people, objects, and activities that fill the heart of your home every day.

how to use this book

This planner will enable home remodelers to feel confident in their choice of appliances, cabinets, storage, and lighting for the kitchen. The planner includes double-page spreads of several kinds to show the options available to anyone planning to update their kitchen. Key features are highlighted here.

planning pages show and describe different types of kitchens, to help you to figure out what you have and what you want

plans offer ideas on where to locate the main kitchen workstations for maximum use of space and ease of working

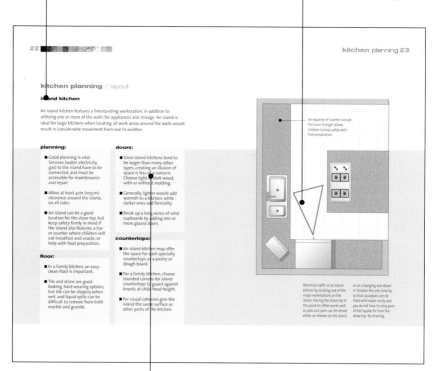

kitchen planning 23

kitchen planning / layout

island kitchen

An island kitchen features a freestanding workstation, in addition to utilizing one or more of the walls for appliances and storage. An island is ideal for large kitchens when locating all work areas around the walls would result in considerable movement from one to another.

planning:

- Good planning is vital. Services (water, electricity, gas) to the island have to be connected, and must be accessible for maintenance and repair.

- Allow at least 42in (105cm) clearance around the island on all sides.

- An island can be a good location for the stove top, but keep safety firmly in mind if the island also features a bar or counter where children will eat breakfast and snacks, or help with food preparation.

floor:

- In a family kitchen, an easy-clean floor is important.

- Tile and stone are good-looking, hard-wearing options, but tile can be slippery when wet, and liquid spills can be difficult to remove from both marble and granite.

doors:

- Since island kitchens tend to be larger than many other types, creating an illusion of space is less of a concern. Choose light or dark wood, with or without molding.

- Generally, lighter woods add warmth to a kitchen, while darker ones add formality.

- Break up a long series of solid cupboards by adding one or more glazed doors.

countertops:

- An island kitchen may offer the space for such specialty countertops as a pastry or dough board.

- For a family kitchen, choose rounded corners for island countertops to guard against knocks at child-head height.

- For visual cohesion give the island the same surface as other parts of the kitchen.

An expanse of counter outside the main triangle allows children to help safely with food preparation

Minimize traffic in an island kitchen by locating one of the major workstations on the island. Placing the stove top in this position often works well, as pots and pans can be stored either on shelves on the island or on a hanging rack above it. Position the sink close by so that saucepans can be filled with water easily, and you do not have to carry pans of hot liquids far from the stove top for draining.

guidelines offer advice on factors to consider when planning, and choosing materials for floors, doors, and countertops

on the left side of each double-page spread are combinations of cabinet doors, counters, and floors

on the right side of each double-page spread are combinations of doors and handles

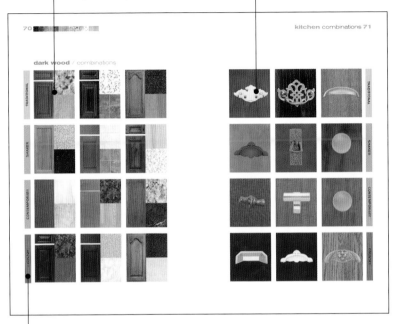

combinations are grouped according to four main themes: traditional, Shaker, contemporary, and country

the style theme of each inspirational photograph is highlighted at the start of the caption

stunning photographs of kitchens—with cabinets, appliances, and accessories in situ—offer ideas to try out in your own space

mix and match

Unique to *Plan Your Kitchen*, the mix-and-match gallery of images enables you to create thousands of combinations of wall cabinets; wall surfaces, including tiling, splashboards, and countertops; base units; and floors. These pages allow you to experiment with different styles, materials, and finishes. You can see instantly, from the comfort of your home, what will work in your space, and then pinpoint what you want.

pages are split into four, allowing individual elements of the room to be considered in turn, and decisions to be made on styles, materials, finishes, and colorways

the top of each cut page features ideas for wall cabinets

wall surfaces, including tiles, splashboards, and countertops, form the second section of the cut pages

base units, including under-counter appliances, are highlighted in the third section of the pages

floors feature at the bottom of each cut page, to complete the look

chapter one

Planning is vital to creating a kitchen that matches your style and meets your needs. Few people have the luxury of starting with a blank canvas and creating a new room from scratch. Most of us have to work with an existing space. This chapter considers the basic types of kitchens, and suggests what you should consider when planning and making your choices for floors, cabinets, and countertops. We also look at safety issues, including safety for children, as well as some common kitchen problems and what you can do to minimize their impact on your design. Some kitchen styles are then introduced: these styles recur throughout the book and will influence your choices for appliances, cabinets, and equipment and gadgets you may be purchasing. Finally, the chapter considers planning one of the most important elements in the kitchen—the lighting.

kitchen planning / layout

one-wall galley kitchen

In a one-wall galley kitchen, all appliances and storage units are positioned along the same wall, so their relationship to each other becomes important. This type of kitchen can work well, particularly when only one person is using it, but it needs more planning if two people want to work together.

planning:

- Create distinct areas for different functions, such as food preparation, cooking, and dish washing. This will help to keep to a minimum the inevitable crossing of paths when two people are working, particularly if the galley is narrow.

- Consider locating the refrigerator near the entrance, so that it can be accessed by others without interfering with the main working areas.

floor:

- Single galleys tend to have a door at each end, so through traffic is common. For this reason, it is wise to install hard-wearing flooring.

- Cost is less likely to be an issue where floor space is limited, so it's worth buying the best flooring you can afford, and it should last for years.

doors:

- Clean lines usually work more effectively than other styles in a single galley. Light wood or laminate helps to create an illusion of space, and will reflect light.

- Consider having storage units custom made so they fit the space exactly.

countertops:

- It is worth considering a movable food preparation stand, such as a butcher block. Not only does this increase the work space, but it also allows food preparation to be carried out without hindering any other work.

- The height of the countertops can be an issue if people of different height are working regularly in the kitchen. Be sure to take this into account when planning and buying.

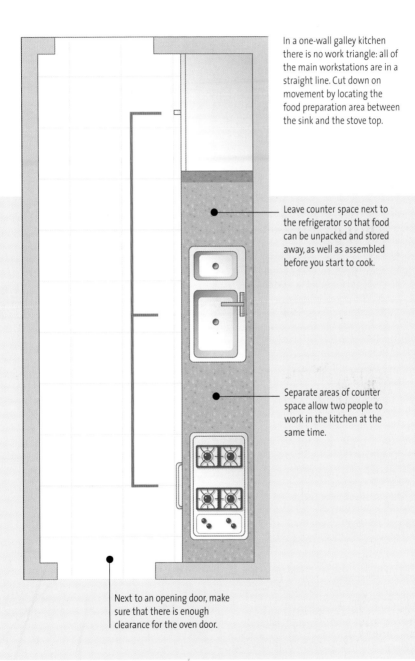

In a one-wall galley kitchen there is no work triangle: all of the main workstations are in a straight line. Cut down on movement by locating the food preparation area between the sink and the stove top.

Leave counter space next to the refrigerator so that food can be unpacked and stored away, as well as assembled before you start to cook.

Separate areas of counter space allow two people to work in the kitchen at the same time.

Next to an opening door, make sure that there is enough clearance for the oven door.

kitchen planning / layout

two-wall galley kitchen

Galley kitchens with workstations on two facing walls are ergonomically ideal, since they provide efficient and simple use of space. Plan storage areas and appliances within areas of specific activity so you can move easily from one side to the other.

planning:

- Two people cooking at one time is easier if the tasks are divided, so one person concentrates on preparing ingredients while the other uses the cooking appliances.

- It may work to keep all of the appliances on one side, and the food preparation areas on the other.

- Make sure that there are storage areas next to the relevant appliance. This avoids unnecessary traffic.

doors:

- Select cabinet doors that are sleek, contemporary, and flush with the cabinets. This maximizes space. Larger doors do not work well in confined spaces.

- If space is tight, replace doors with roller shades that need no clearance.

- Small galleys will look larger if you use a unified color scheme and open shelving instead of wall cabinets.

floor:

- Choose a high-quality floor for visual appeal, easy cleaning, and extended durability.

- Suitable materials include wood, which always looks stylish, or ceramic tiles, which give an enormous range in terms of color and price.

countertops:

- Slate and granite look stylish, are very hard-wearing, and last for years.

- Where space between the two galley walls is greater than 48in (120cm), install a deeper countertop that can double as a breakfast bar.

When well planned, a two-wall galley can be ideal. Locate two main workstations on one wall and one on the other. Avoid having two workstations face each other, so that two people do not have to work back-to-back. Position the dishwasher and garbage receptacle close to the sink so that it is easy to clear leftover food from plates and load the dishwasher.

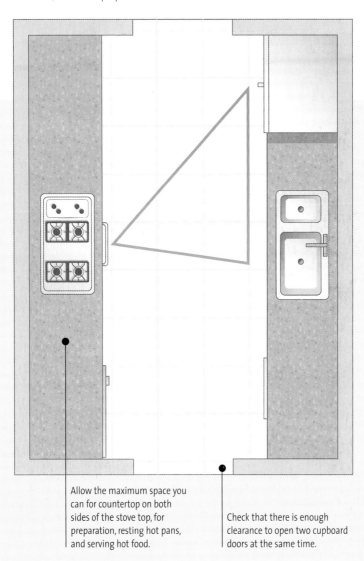

Allow the maximum space you can for countertop on both sides of the stove top, for preparation, resting hot pans, and serving hot food.

Check that there is enough clearance to open two cupboard doors at the same time.

kitchen planning / layout

U-shaped kitchen

In a U-shaped kitchen one workstation can be on each of three walls. This creates a versatile and efficient design where more than one person can work with ease. A big advantage is that there is unlikely to be through traffic, so people working in the kitchen are not disturbed.

planning:

- Ideally you need an overall floor area of 8ft x 8ft (2.4m x 2.4m) to make this type of kitchen work. This allows space in the central area for two people to work.

- If wall space is at a premium, consider removing radiators and fitting under-floor heating.

- If your refrigerator is near a corner, make sure the door is hung on the appropriate side, so that it won't bang into low-level cabinets on the adjoining arm of the U.

floor:

- In a small U, noise can be a problem, so marble, tile, or stone may not be the best choices. Select softer options such as treated wood, vinyl, or laminate.

- Choose a hard-wearing floor. Although there is no through traffic, two or more people working in this type of kitchen create wear and tear.

doors:

- Light woods and laminates will reflect light, which can be good if the corners of the kitchen always tend to look dark and gloomy.

- Add to the illusion of space by breaking up a series of solid doors with one or more glazed doors, or with some open shelves.

- Make sure all doors in the corners have enough clearance to open freely.

countertops:

- This type of kitchen has the potential for long series of countertop, so cost is likely to be a factor. But remember that the most expensive materials such as granite will usually need replacing less often than cheaper options.

- If you want marble for pastry and dough making, consider inserting a block into a cheaper countertop.

A corner of the U is an ideal space for a microwave oven, or for a small TV.

As a guide, allow a minimum of 24in (60cm) between the refrigerator and the sink.

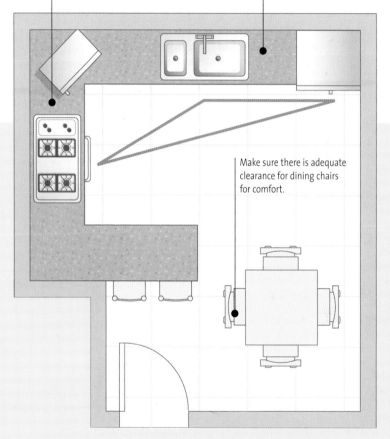

Make sure there is adequate clearance for dining chairs for comfort.

In this design you may have the option of spacing the three main workstations of stove top, refrigerator, and sink equidistantly for maximum efficiency. If the U is narrow, do not locate two workstations directly opposite each other. The ample countertop in this design means that small appliances such as a toaster or coffee machine can be accommodated on the countertop itself rather than being stored away, but aim to keep the kitchen as clutter free as possible. Store little used items in the deep corner cupboards, which are more difficult to access.

kitchen planning / layout

G-shaped kitchen

Essentially a U-shaped kitchen with the addition of a peninsula or "leg" of units or appliances, a G-shaped kitchen offers lots of space, as well as versatility. The work area can be spread out, allowing more than one person to work with ease. This design is ideal where lots of storage is needed.

planning:

- You need a greater floor area than for a U-shaped kitchen to make this design work. Make sure that the extra leg does not impede work flow between areas.

- Consider separating the stove top and oven, as well as installing two sinks, so that two people can prepare and cook food at the same time.

- Make good use of corners by choosing cabinets designed for them. Ensure that an open dishwasher does not impede access to storage units.

floor:

- If this is a family kitchen, choose the softer options, such as laminates and vinyl. Although they wear less well than harder surfaces, their warmth and ease of maintenance makes them ideal where children are concerned and in areas of heavy traffic.

doors:

- Lighter woods and laminates may be a good choice if you want to keep the kitchen light and bright; pale colors also make it easier to see and remove dirt.

- Make maximum use of space by adding hooks for utensils to the ends of a series of cupboards.

countertops:

- Like the U-shaped kitchen, this design has long expanses of countertop, so your choices may have cost implications. However, the most expensive options are more likely to be harder wearing.

- Choose easy-maintenance counters if you do a lot of cooking. Unmopped spills can damage granite, marble, and other surfaces.

This shape usually affords one or more lengthy expanses of countertop, separating food preparation and serving well.

Positioning the sink in a corner is a good use of space. Corner cupboards can be "dead" space; here it holds all of the plumbing and garbage disposal pipes.

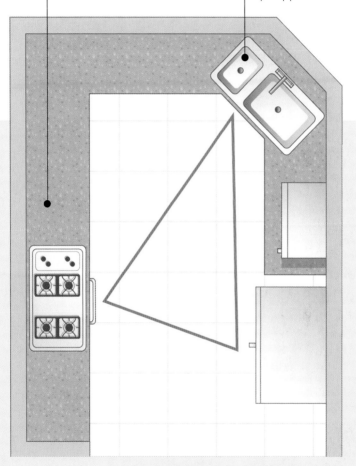

A G-shaped kitchen is a good option if you have the space. For a large family, where maximum storage is vital, this is one of the best designs, and it is usually possible to include at least a small bar or table area where children can eat breakfasts and snacks. The lengthy expanse of countertop means that the three major workstations can be located for maximum efficiency, and enables two or more people to work in the kitchen at the same time in comfort.

kitchen planning / layout

L-shaped kitchen

The adjacent walls in an L-shaped kitchen form a natural work triangle. This kind of space is very flexible and adaptable to a whole range of layouts. It has the added advantage that a seating area can easily be incorporated into the free space.

planning:

- This plan is ideal for a small dining area where two people can eat together comfortably.

- The kitchen is not just a dedicated food preparation area. One person is able to cook while the other does something else.

- Make sure the countertop at the inside angle of your L doesn't become dead space because it's too hard to reach. If this is the case, look for a lazy Susan to hold items so they are visible with one spin.

floor:

- Very hard materials absorb no sound, and if used over a large area, often tend to create a noisy working environment and so should be avoided.

- If the kitchen has a dining area where you will want to chat, consider a soft-tiled or linoleum floor that will absorb sound.

doors:

- The L-shaped kitchen is more open than a galley and may be lighter, so your choice of cabinet doors can be more flexible.

- When they are in a corner, the far reaches of cabinet interiors can be difficult to access. When you choose your cabinets, look for doors that are hinged so they look like two doors, but unfold in one easy movement.

countertops:

- Consider low-maintenance finishes for countertops so you can spend less time cleaning them.

- If you keep wines, create a rack at the end of a series of countertops in the awkward open-ended space that an L-shaped kitchen often tends to include.

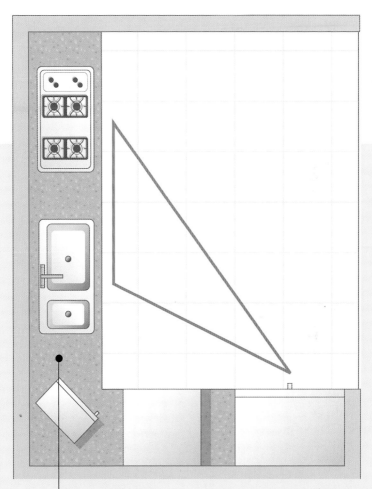

Allow space between the microwave and sink to drain liquids from foods as they are removed from the microwave.

An L-shaped design allows you to space out the three main workstations. You could add a movable food preparation area, such as a butcher block, so that more than one person can work at the same time.

kitchen planning / layout

island kitchen

An island kitchen features a freestanding workstation, in addition to utilizing one or more of the walls for appliances and storage. An island is ideal for large kitchens when locating all work areas around the walls would result in considerable movement from one to another.

planning:

- Good planning is vital. Services (water, electricity, gas) to the island have to be connected, and must be accessible for maintenance and repair.

- Allow at least 42in (105cm) clearance around the island, on all sides.

- An island can be a good location for the stove top, but keep safety firmly in mind if the island also features a bar or counter where children will eat breakfast and snacks, or help with food preparation.

floor:

- In a family kitchen, an easy-clean floor is important.

- Tile and stone are good-looking, hard-wearing options, but tile can be slippery when wet, and liquid spills can be difficult to remove from both marble and granite.

doors:

- Since island kitchens tend to be larger than many other types, creating an illusion of space is less of a concern. Choose light or dark wood, with or without molding.

- Generally, lighter woods add warmth to a kitchen, while darker ones add formality.

- Break up a long series of solid cupboards by adding one or more glazed doors.

countertops:

- An island kitchen may offer the space for such specialty countertops as a pastry or dough board.

- For a family kitchen, choose rounded corners for island countertops to guard against knocks at child-head height.

- For visual cohesion give the island the same surface as other parts of the kitchen.

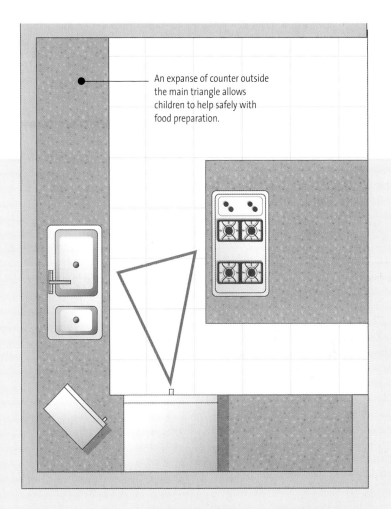

An expanse of counter outside the main triangle allows children to help safely with food preparation.

Minimize traffic in an island kitchen by locating one of the major workstations on the island. Placing the stove top in this position often works well, as pots and pans can be stored either on shelves on the island or on a hanging rack above it. Position the sink close by so that saucepans can be filled with water easily, and you do not have to carry pans of hot liquids far from the stove top for draining.

kitchen planning / ergonomics

In the simplest terms, ergonomics makes life easier and safer for people working in the kitchen. At its heart is the working triangle (see below): the distance between sink, refrigerator, and stove top should not be too great. Ergonomics also covers such factors as the height of cupboards and work surfaces, and the positioning of appliances relative to the three main work stations. In a carefully planned kitchen, you do not have to lift heavy equipment over long distances or travel far to get what you need.

working triangle

The concept of the working triangle underpins good kitchen design. Essentially the three major workstations of sink, stove top or range, and refrigerator should form a triangle. Measured from the center of each of these stations, the perimeter line of the triangle should be at least 12ft (3.6m) in length and no more than 26ft (8m) for maximum efficiency. Similarly, each side of the triangle should measure at least 4ft (1.2m) in length and no more than 9ft (2.75m).

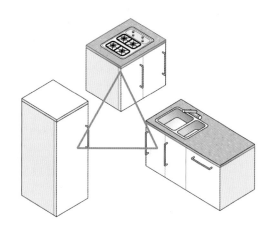

safe space

It is generally suggested that aisles in the main working areas should be at least 42in (105cm) wide in a one-person kitchen, and 48in (120cm) in a two-person kitchen, but be guided by the size of your appliances. If you have a large-size refrigerator, make sure that the door can open fully without knocking into any cupboard or appliance. A door that is half ajar is a safety hazard.

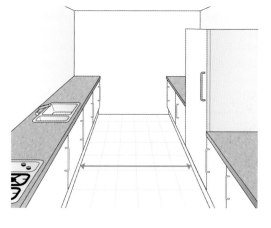

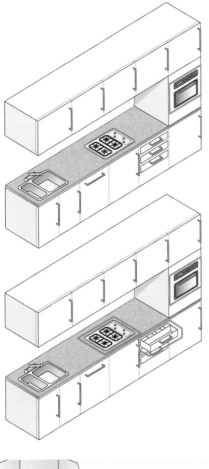

ovens & stove tops

An oven needs an area of clear floor space at least 30in x 48in (75cm x 120cm) in front of it. An eye-level oven is back-friendly for the cook, and safer if there are children in the house. If the oven sits in a tall unit, this should be positioned at one end of a series of units, rather than interrupting a series of base and wall units.

Allow at least 24in (60cm) of work surface to one side of the stove top and the oven so that you can rest hot pots and pans removed from the heat source. A drawer between oven and stove top is useful for storing cooking utensils within easy reach of both appliances.

ventilator hoods

Center your ventilator hood over the stove top and position it a minimum of 25in (65cm) and a maximum of 30in (75cm) above it: use the higher figure for a gas stove top. For a standard range or stove top, the hood should have a cubic feet per minute (cfm) rating of at least 150; if your stove top includes a griddle or grill unit, the cfm should be higher.

kitchen planning / ergonomics

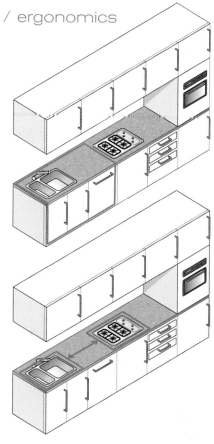

sink position

Place the dishwasher next to the sink so that prewashing plates before loading the dishwasher is easy. If the dishwasher is located under a countertop, you have a place to unload the dishes.

Position the sink at least 24in (60cm) from the stove top. This allows space for food preparation within easy reach of running water, as well as providing a short distance to carry pots and pans full of water for heating, and hot liquid for emptying.

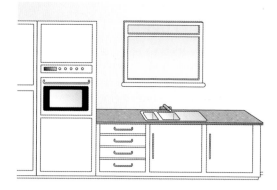

Positioning the sink under a window serves two main purposes. During the day, it allows tasks to be carried out at the sink in natural light so that it is easy to see if pots and pans are clean. Second, it gives the person standing at the sink an interesting view. Ensure that when it is in position, the faucet will not impede opening the window.

dining & bar measurements

Most people choose to have some sort of eating area in the kitchen, even if they do not have space for a full-size dining table. There are two main considerations when planning eating spaces. First, ensure enough space around tables and seating for free movement and to avoid feeling hemmed in. Second, choose seating of an appropriate height for the table or bar counter.

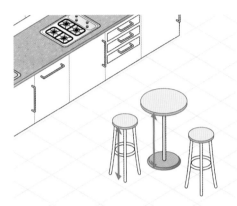

LEFT Knees must fit under bar counters in comfort. For a bar height of 44in (110cm) choose stools around 30in (75cm) high; for a bar height of 36in (90cm) stools should be around 24in (60cm) high.

BELOW To dine in the kitchen, ensure a free space of 48in (120cm) in all directions so diners are not cramped, and allow enough space for the cook to serve the food.

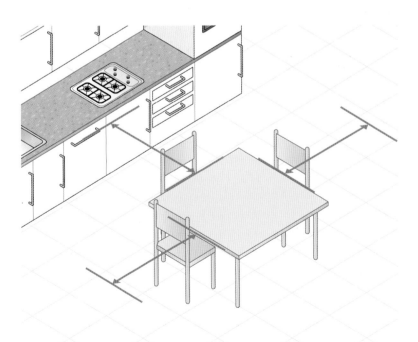

kitchen planning / kitchen safety

It is vital to keep safety in mind when you are planning your kitchen. More accidents happen here than in any other room in the house, because there are more hazards than are found in any other room. The main causes for concern are fire, both prevention and dealing with it if one does break out; children, whose natural curiosity and enthusiasm to be involved in everything can prove hazardous; and inherent dangers in what is stored in the kitchen, and how.

GENERAL SAFETY

■ Plan adequate lighting at all times of the day and night so you can get around the kitchen and see what you are doing. Be aware of potential dark spots, such as in the corners under cupboards, and either install good lighting, or use these dark areas for the microwave or a TV.

■ When planning the electric outlets, be sure to install enough sockets so you do not overload them. You must get circuits for large appliances installed by a professional electrician.

■ Install a lockable drawer for sharp knives, or store them in a knife block. Wash knives as soon as you finish using them and put them away. This is doubly important if you have children.

■ Set aside a lockable cupboard to hold all household cleaning products and other chemicals. Always read caution labels and, if possible, purchase products that are less caustic and dangerous.

■ When considering possible flooring materials, take into account how slippery they might be when wet. Be prepared to mop spills immediately.

■ Make sure electrical, plumbing, and ventilation ducts, pipes, and cables are easy to access for repairs and servicing, and that you know how to turn off the main water inlet and main electricity supply if it becomes necessary.

■ If you are planning fabric drapes and other flammable materials, including plants, locate them with care: they must be nowhere near the stove top.

CHILDREN

The only way to keep children safe in the kitchen is not to let them in, but this is not practical in most families. These precautions should help to minimize the impact of potential hazards.

- Plan an area away from the working triangle where children can play. Young children may be happy in a playpen for a time; older children can cut cookies, or do some drawing, well out of the way of hazards, but still within your sight.

- Choose an oven with a child-safety lock so children cannot open the door. Check that the oven ventilation system keeps the door as cool as possible.

- Children can pull a drawer out of its housing and get hurt when the contents spill out. Install locks to ensure that drawers cannot be completely removed, no matter how hard they are pulled.

- Cupboard doors that can be opened easily can trap a child's fingers. In addition, the contents of the cupboard may not be child friendly. Fit cupboard locks to ensure that children cannot gain access to the contents.

- A stove top guard ensures that a child cannot pull a pan of hot food or liquid from the stove top, or get a burn from the ring. For added safety, use only the back burners whenever possible.

- Once children can toddle, be sure there is nothing in the kitchen they could use to clamber into a danger zone, such as a chair that can lead to access to the stove top or countertop.

FIRE SAFETY IN THE KITCHEN

- Kitchens can be fire hazards: faulty appliances, naked flames, and a moment's inattention by the cook all pose fire risks.

- Most kitchen fires are caused by deep fat fryers. Never leave a deep fat fryer unattended. Ideally buy a model with a thermostat (these cannot overheat). Fill the fryer no more than one-third full. Dry food before putting it in. If the oil starts to smoke, turn the fryer off and leave to cool. If the fryer does catch fire, turn off the power. Never use water on an oil fire: you could create a fireball.

- Install hooks or rails to hold dish towels and pot holders. A dish towel or pot holder left on the stove top can ignite fast.

- Keep appliance cords away from the cooker and from water, and do not allow them to trail. Check regularly for wear. Avoid overloading sockets with plugs, and do not run extension cords on the floor. Install ground fault circuit interrupter receptacles near sinks and any other wet areas.

- Consider buying self-cleaning appliances, where possible. A buildup of grease on the stove top, grill, or rotisserie, or in the oven, can lead to a fire.

- Install a dry powder or light foam fire extinguisher in the kitchen and know how to use it. If in any doubt about tackling a fire, don't. Turn off the heat if possible, leave the room, close the door, and dial 911.

kitchen planning / what do you want?

Before you start to define the style that is right for you, spend some time thinking about how you use this room. For many families, the kitchen is the center of the home, and its functions extend far beyond meal preparation. For other people, however, this is still primarily a place to cook. Think about whether you want to entertain in the kitchen. Consider maintenance, too. If you do not spend much time there, chances are you will not want to spend a lot of time keeping it clean and tidy, so low-maintenance styles may

suit you. Think, too, about what you want to store here: this will help you to work out how many cabinets you are likely to need. In turn, this may have an influence on your style choices. The most beautiful cabinets can be overpowering if there are simply too many of them in one room.

the four styles

For ease of use in this planner, kitchen furniture and accessories are grouped into four major styles: traditional, Shaker, contemporary, and country. Traditional kitchens never go out of style. They are characterized by materials such as wood or black-and-white tile flooring, natural wood or white cabinets with inset or raised panels, and

SHAKER

- The colors used for painted cabinets in Shaker kitchens were natural shades such as turkey red, blue, and dark green.

- Built-in cupboards and drawers were common, with a place for every item used in the kitchen.

- For doors and drawers choose models with no molding and fit plain handles to them.

kitchen planning / what do you want?

CONTEMPORARY

■ Up-to-the-minute appliances, such as a mirror-door oven or a glass-fronted refrigerator allow you to see the contents without opening the door, so you save on energy. You do, however, have to keep the interior of the appliance tidy.

marble countertops. The color scheme is often earthy, while floral motifs are common. The choice of knobs and handles is limitless. A hanging pot rack is good finishing touch.

The clean lines, utility, and durability of Shaker designs make Shaker-style kitchens popular. There was no ornamentation in Shaker pieces, so if you are attempting this look, choose plain cabinets with functional handles and drawer pulls. Tables and chairs should also be unadorned and functional.

Contemporary kitchens are spacious and sleek. Cabinets feature clean lines with no molding or other decoration, in bright colors such as blues and reds. Walls are likely to be white and appliances black, white, or stainless steel.

Country style is about comfort and warmth. Unpolished wood is common for cabinets; the floor may be stone, and the walls cream or white. You could consider installing a range for both cooking and warmth, and opt for some free-standing furniture such as a dresser or hutch.

COUNTRY

- Fabrics in mixed patterns and colorways enhance a country-style kitchen.

- Various warm-colored woods can be combined in this type of kitchen: you could choose mismatched but even-toned chairs for this look.

kitchen planning / dealing with problems

Few kitchens are ideal blank canvases on which you can start to design your new room. In practice, when kitchen planning, you will have to work around limitations or solve problems before you can get started. Remember that there is very little you cannot do—or get done for you—but changing some things will cost more in time and money, as well as general hassle. Be aware, too, of planning regulations: if you need permission to make the changes you want, this could add time to your schedule. Problems and constraints generally fall into two categories: structural and functional. Here are some of the most common problems and possible ways around them.

STRUCTURAL PROBLEMS

■ Chimney structures and the alcoves they create are part of the design of the room. They are difficult to remove. If your heart is set on a chimney's going, but the chimney continues onto higher floors, you must install a steel beam to support the upper floors. It is easier by far to treat a chimney structure as a classic period feature, and either cut into it and use it for storage, or fill it with a cast-iron range to provide a warm focal point for the room, as it did in the past.

■ Uneven floors are common, especially in older properties. The problem may be that the floor rises and dips, or the corner may be a different level than the main part of the floor. If the floor is concrete, it is easy to apply a leveling scree, and use that as your new subfloor. Alternatively, choose base units with adjustable feet, and hide the unevenness behind a baseboard.

■ If your kitchen is not on the ground floor or in the basement, check the weight of any pieces you are planning on buying. The floor joists may need to be strengthened to take the weight.

■ For the sake of safety, wall and base cabinets must be attached to the walls. However, if you have drywall or stud walls, these may not be sufficiently robust to support the weight of the cupboards. Locate the studs and use these as your anchor points. If they are in the wrong place, you can anchor braces to the studs, and attach your cabinets to the braces.

■ Uneven walls are common in older homes, or the wall covering, such as tiles, may be broken, chipped, or dirty. The easiest way around broken or chipped tiles is to fill any large breaks with scraps, then tile over the old ones. You can line damaged plaster walls with drywall and use that as your base; this is a cheaper and quicker option than trying to replaster and gives good results.

■ It is very easy to alter the way a door opens and closes, and far less hassle than cutting a new doorway.

■ The wall above a new window needs the support of a steel beam.

POWERING STOVE TOPS & OVENS

■ Electric stove tops and ovens can use a lot of power. If you are planning a major kitchen remodel, you may need to calculate whether you have enough capacity for your electrical wish list.

■ Homes were generally built with 150-amp capacity, although some had only 100 amps. What this means is that a stove top or oven using 50 amps can take 1/3 to 1/4 of the house's supply. Generally this is not a problem, since very few appliances use a great deal of power: lights, TVs, and even computers are low users, compared with a stove top or oven.

■ Get a written quotation on the differences in cost between 30-, 40-, and 50-amp circuits for your stove top and oven. Plan ahead: you may want to install an electric cooker at some point (or sell the house to someone who wants to).

■ You want the highest amperage you can afford. Check with your contractor or electrician on the difference in price between a 30-amp circuit (realistically, the minimum you need) and higher capacities. Ask about the impact of higher loads on the wiring of the house as a whole. Ask the power company about the nominal and assured minimum voltage levels for 230-volt circuits, and get this in writing if you can.

■ Calculate the minimum power you'll be able to supply to your cooking unit. If you have a 30-amp circuit and a minimum of 200 volts, you have 30 x 200 = 6,000 watts (or 6kW) available. Get a statement in writing from the manufacturer on the maximum power that any unit you are interested in can supply with each element set to its maximum. Then be sure that is within the limit you have calculated.

WATER & WASTE

■ Waste pipes can be difficult to move yourself, and add considerable expense to the job if you employ someone else to do the work. Take their position into account when planning where to position the sink and dishwasher.

■ If you do decide to move them, check where they enter the room. It may be possible to reroute them under the floor, rather than run in new ones. Take this factor into account if you are going to be installing an island unit needing drainage.

■ Make sure all service inlets to the kitchen are accessible. Hide them under a removable baseboard, if necessary.

UPDATE YOUR PIPE SYSTEM?

■ If you are remodeling the kitchen of an older property, your plumbing contractor will probably want to do a thorough inspection before agreeing to take on the job. Your plumber will want to be sure that, if there are any outdated components like brass or lead pipes, in your system, he knows how to handle them. Your plumber will also know about technological developments that might be useful to you, such as flexible piping.

kitchen planning / lighting

The main function of most kitchens is still the preparation and cooking of food, and clearing up afterward. For this reason, the major workstations of stove top and sink—as well as countertops where food is prepared and served—require good illumination. Kitchen lighting should also contribute to kitchen safety, so corners need to be lit, as do any areas where spills are likely and spaces where children's toys might be left to create a tripping hazard. Kitchens today are about more than food, however. In many households the kitchen is the center of family activity, where people gravitate to talk about the day, do homework, pay bills, and read the newspaper. These other functions also need to be factored into your lighting considerations.

light and shadow
In a small kitchen, a ceiling light may be all that is necessary to provide well-diffused general lighting for moving around, looking into drawers and cupboards, and performing general tasks. The drawback is that at the main workstations you may be working in your own shadow. The way to avoid this is to add supplemental task lighting. Generally, there are four areas where this is necessary: over the stove top, above the countertops, at the

ambient lighting
The general background light level in a room is known as ambient lighting. Ambient light makes the room pleasant to be in.

■ Remember that a skylight or door to a yard, garden, or patio will add to the level of ambient light.

■ Fluorescent strip lights in the ceiling cast light downward and outward, for balanced light.

■ It is useful to be able to change ambient lighting by fitting a dimmer switch on an ambient light so you can adjust it at different times of day.

accent lighting

To highlight what you want to be noticed, you need accent lighting. This may pick out an architectural detail or a collection of antique china, or simply a lovely range or hutch.

- Use low-voltage strip lighting inside glazed cabinets to draw attention to their contents.

- Halogen spotlights or track lighting can be used to pick out cabinet moldings or wood grain.

- Aim a halogen spotlight or track of lights on a dining area table to improve illumination while you are eating.

task lighting

As the name suggests, task lighting is focused on one or more specific spots where key kitchen tasks are carried out. You have various options available to you.

- Under-cabinet lighting illuminates the countertop without casting shadows across it.

- Fluorescent under-cabinet lights are economical to run and stay cool.

- For dining areas, add a pendant light to hang 24-30in (60-75cm) above the table. Fit a dimmer switch so the light can be lowered when the meal is over.

kitchen planning / lighting

sink, and over breakfast bars and island units. A track light set over the sink will provide good illumination; recessed down lights also work here, as well as over the stove top. For added light on the countertops, install under cabinet lighting Choose energy-efficient strips at least two-thirds the width of the cabinet. Installing these at the back cuts down on glare. A pendant over a bar or island gives good light for reading, homework, and other family business.

creating atmosphere

To create an atmospheric lighting scheme, add lights in the appropriate places. One of the simplest ways to create atmosphere is to add a dimmer switch to a pendant light used over a bar or island unit. The light can be set on high when work is being carried out, and dimmed for dining and entertaining. Using spotlights to accent room features adds warmth and creates a pleasant atmosphere.

BELOW In this lighting scheme, recessed ceiling spotlights provide ambient light. Task lighting over the major kitchen workstations illuminates them when in use, and spotlights provide good background lighting for safety when the kitchen is not in use.

LEFT Adding a light to the ventilator hood is a good way of ensuring that the stove top is adequately illuminated, while task lighting over the sink enables anyone who is working there to make sure that pots and pans are clean.

BELOW When the task lighting is on, key workstations are well illuminated. A good mix of ambient, task, and accent lighting works best in most kitchens, especially in large spaces where functions are well separated.

kitchen planning / lighting

lighting checklist

You should plan, early in the design process, where you are going to place your major sources of light. Once you have reached a decision on your overall style theme, use these guidelines to help you to achieve the look you want to fit with your style.

TRADITIONAL

- Dangling pendant lights enhance a traditional dining area or nook.

- Choose under-cabinet lighting to illuminate countertops: these lights can be hidden by a pelmet.

- Freestanding antique lamps can work well in this style of kitchen.

- Lights positioned on top of cabinets and shining on the ceiling will send a soft light over the whole room, without being obtrusive.

SHAKER

- Choose functional light fittings: good task lighting will enhance the clean lines of the Shaker look.

- Recessed lights are functional, efficient, and unobtrusive.

- Avoid elaborate pendants, ultra-modern fixtures, and patterned lamp shades. For a colored shade, choose traditional colors such as red, blue, or green.

- For down lights, white trims with a white baffle often blend with the ceiling better than other trims and are less obtrusive.

CONTEMPORARY

- Halogen or xenon spotlights add to the up-to-the-minute look of a contemporary kitchen. Xenon provides a long-lived incandescent light that can be dimmed.

- If you are using black or stainless steel in your design, consider industrial rather than domestic light fittings.

- Choose finishes such as nickel and chrome for light fittings that are going to remain visible.

- A sculptural lighting piece can work well as a focal point.

COUNTRY

- Fluorescent strips, although useful, can be too harsh for the warm, cozy feel of a country kitchen. Look for a color temperature in the region of 3,000–3,500 Kelvin.

- Several lamps, dotted around the kitchen, can enhance the feeling of warmth and comfort.

- Focus accent lighting on any piece of antique furniture or china, or use it to highlight the grain or molding of wooden cabinets.

- Stainless steel pendant lights can work well in this type of kitchen.

chapter two

Your choice of appliances can make the difference between a kitchen that is a huge success and one that does not work as you hoped and wished. Appliances are expensive and should last for several years, so getting them right is important. In this chapter both large and smaller items are considered. Your largest purchases are likely to be for your refrigeration needs, including freezing, and for cooking, so this chapter presents a variety of refrigerators, freezers, and refrigerator/freezers, together with a selection of ovens, stove tops, and ranges. In each case, dimensions are included so that you can tell immediately if a product is appropriate for your needs. In between the product shots are photographs of different appliances in real kitchens to help you to decide whether an item is right for you.

appliances / general considerations

There are several factors to consider when choosing appliances for your kitchen. Appliances can be costly, so it is worth spending time over your choices. The first factor is size, which covers both physical size—how much floor and wall space you will need to accommodate the appliance—and internal capacity. If you have a growing family, chances are that bigger is going to be best for appliances like freezers and refrigerators. Similarly, if you are an enthusiastic cook who likes entertaining, you may need the flexibility offered by more than one oven, as well as a dishwasher that can accommodate up to 12 place settings in one wash.

power and specifications

Power is your next consideration: do you have gas or electricity? If you do not have what you need, how easy is it going to be to change, and how much is that going to add to your budget? Particularly for ovens and stove

TRADITIONAL	SHAKER
■ A cast-iron range may be a good choice for a traditional kitchen, with major manufacturers producing ranges in different colorways. These colors may not be strictly authentic for any historical period, but they will blend nicely with traditional palettes.	■ An original Shaker kitchen would have had no appliances apart from a solid-fuel range. If you want a Shaker-style theme, either hide your high-tech appliances behind plain but graceful timber panels, or cling to the Shaker spirit by choosing white appliances with the minimum of adornment.
■ Black, white, and cream are safe choices, so choose one of these and play with color on the walls, as well as in furnishings and textiles.	■ For authenticity, cast-iron ranges should be black. Those willing to compromise a little could choose cream or white, but anything else is too colorful.
■ Find inspiration from the past by sticking with standard white appliances and creating a retro theme around them. You could suggest the 1950s with black-and-white-checkered flooring and a black-and-pastel palette.	■ Ahead of their time, the Shakers sometimes installed simple, separate griddles and deep fryers in their kitchens (in black), so these modern items would work well in a Shaker-themed room.
■ Try to steer clear of anything trendy or fashion-centered. By definition what's "in" today is "out" tomorrow, and the beauty of a traditional kitchen is that it does not date.	

tops, do you have a particular preference in how you cook? The product specifications will tell you what is needed in terms of power to run the appliance safely and to the best effect. The specifications may also give an ecological rating: this lets you know how energy efficient the appliance is. Look for factors such as the ability to wash a half-load of dishes, or to cook a meal in one oven or by using only the stove top.

looking good

The third factor to bear in mind is your overall style and color scheme. The days when almost all kitchen appliances were finished in white are long gone. The options available now are enormous in terms of materials and colors. Many appliances are available as under-counter models, with their exteriors hidden behind standard cabinet doors. If this is your choice, colors and materials may be less important to you, but check the dimensions carefully to be sure they will fit: standard-sized appliances may be too wide or deep to sit inside a standard-sized cabinet.

CONTEMPORARY

- Architecturally modern kitchens demand appliances that are white, black, or stainless steel. Glass doors suit the look perfectly, and allow you to see inside ranges and refrigerators without opening the door.

- This style allows your imagination free rein. Colored appliances look great in these schemes; they are often expensive, but they're bright and unusual and are likely to bring a smile to your face every time you use them.

- Whichever colors and materials you choose, opt for appliances with clean, sleek lines and a complete absence of fake period styling.

COUNTRY

- If you favor wood finishes, look for appliances that will fit under counters or in wall housings to match the rest of the cabinets.

- Cast-iron ranges offer the warmth and comfort many people want in a country kitchen, as well as providing a good focal point.

- Whites and creams are good choices for country kitchens, so opt for appliances in these colors and add warm accents elsewhere.

- Mismatched furniture and appliances add a great deal to the unself-conscious charm of a country kitchen. In fact, obsessive matching of all the elements— equipment, accessories, fabrics— would compromise the look.

appliances / refrigerators

DIMENSIONS
H68⅝ x W35⅞ x D33⅝
(H1,742 x W910 x D855)
CAPACITY
Refrigerator 17.51 cu ft (496 liters)
Freezer 7.08 cu ft (200 liters)
FINISH
White / Stainless steel

● This model features slide-out, adjustable, split shelves; meat bin; vegetable crisper; automatic ice maker; and chilled water dispenser in the refrigerator, and removable shelves in the freezer. The stainless steel finish option would be suitable for a contemporary kitchen.

DIMENSIONS
H66¾ x W27¾ x D28⅞
(H1,695 x W680 x D734)
CAPACITY
Refrigerator 13.63 cu ft (386 liters)
Freezer 3.24 cu ft (93 liters)
FINISH
White / Stainless steel

● With a top freezer above a large-capacity refrigerator, this model is available in white or stainless steel finishes: white works in traditional kitchens, stainless steel in more contemporary designs. Features include adjustable shelves, humidity control, leveling front feet and rear rollers, and either-side door opening.

DIMENSIONS
H66³/₄ x W31 x D28⁷/₈
(H1,695 x W790 x D734)
CAPACITY
Refrigerator 12.01 cu ft (340 liters)
Freezer 3.99 cu ft (113 liters)
FINISH
White / Stainless steel

● Having a bottom freezer with large-capacity refrigerator on top, this model is available in stainless steel or white finishes: choose white for a traditional scheme. It includes door alarms ando humidity control, and is frost free. The door can be hung on either right or left.

DIMENSIONS
H69⁷/₈ x W35⁷/₈ x D26³/₄
(H1,775 x W911 x D678)
CAPACITY
20 cu ft (566 liters)
FINISH
Black / White / Stainless steel

● Practical for smaller spaces and island kitchens, the doors of this French-door-style refrigerator require minimum space to open fully. The full-depth freezer drawer at the bottom pulls out. Features of the refrigerator include glass shelves, salad crisper, egg caddy, and door bins.

appliances / refrigerators

DIMENSIONS
H83³/₄ x W48 x D24
(H2,127 x W1,219 x D609)
CAPACITY
Refrigerator 18.3 cu ft (518 liters)
Freezer 12.4 cu ft (351 liters)
FINISH
White / Stainless steel / Custom

 With side-by-side refrigerator and freezer,
● this model is available with different
● combinations of internal storage to meet
different requirements. It can also be
supplied with trim to hold customized door
panels to match existing kitchen cabinets,
making it suitable for most kitchen styles.

DIMENSIONS
H69³/₄ x W35¹/₂ x D35¹/₄
(H1,772 x W900 x D894)
CAPACITY
Refrigerator 15.5 cu ft (439 liters)
Freezer 10.1 cu ft (286 liters)
FINISH
Stainless steel

● This model is designed to dispense cold drinks
fast. The refrigerator also features extra-wide
slide-out glass shelves, a crisper, clear meat
and snack bins, and a can rack. The freezer
includes two tilt-out door bins and two tall
baskets. An ice dispenser is fitted into the door,
and the handles are full length for ease of use.

DIMENSIONS
H83³/₈ x W42 x D25¹/₄
(H2,108 x W1,068 x D641)
CAPACITY
26 cu ft (736 liters)
FINISH
Stainless steel / Custom

● Available in stainless steel or with trim to
● hold custom cabinet doors (to work in most
● styles of kitchen), this fridge/freezer is a side-
by-side model with ice-water dispenser. It
includes two temperature zones to maximize
efficient food storage, maintains temperature
to within one degree, and also monitors use
to determine the best time for defrosting.

DIMENSIONS
H83³/₄ x W48 x D24
(H2,127 x W1,219 x D609)
CAPACITY
Refrigerator 18.3 cu ft (518 liters)
Freezer 11.8 cu ft (334 liters)
FINISH
White / Stainless steel / Custom

● With side-by-side refrigerator and freezer,
● this model can also be supplied with trim to
● hold customized door panels to match
existing kitchen cabinets. As such, it is
suitable for most kitchen styles. It is available
with several combinations of internal storage
to meet different requirements, and features
an external ice-water dispenser.

appliances / refrigerator/freezers

CONTEMPORARY

ABOVE Sleek and stylish, large stainless steel refrigerators look good in loft-style spaces.

CONTEMPORARY

OPPOSITE Iridium is durable and resistant to finger marks. This fridge/freezer is ideal in any modern urban setting.

TRADITIONAL

LEFT This refrigerator/freezer dispenses ice and cold drinks, from a closed door so the cold interior is not affected.

appliances / refrigerator/freezers

COUNTRY

ABOVE This unique style statement is a mix of plain country materials, surfaces, and detailing, with jazzy colors and unmistakably urban appliances including a vast, shiny, and practical refrigerator/freezer.

TRADITIONAL

LEFT Classic paneled cabinets in warm, light wood set a traditional scene in which black countertops form a visual link with a sleek-lined refrigerator/freezer, which incorporates a low drawer instead of a hinged door.

CONTEMPORARY

BELOW As well as clean modern styling, this white refrigerator/freezer offers an ice-water dispenser mounted on the outside.

appliances / dishwashers

DIMENSIONS H34'/₂ x W23'/₂ x D22'/₂
(H879 x W595 x D570)
WATER CONSUMPTION 8 quarts (8 liters)
FINISH Stainless steel

● A double-drawer dishwasher, this model has
● child locks, nine wash programs, and space
  for long-stemmed glasses and 24 full-size
  dinner plates.

DIMENSIONS H34'/₂ x W23'/₂ x D22'/₂
(H879 x W595 x D570)
WATER CONSUMPTION 8 quarts (8 liters)
FINISH Stainless steel / Black

● This model has two independent
● dishwashing drawers, and can take up
  to 24 11'/₂in (290mm) dinner plates.

DIMENSIONS H16 x W23'/₂ x D22'/₂
(H409 x W595 x D570)
WATER CONSUMPTION 8 quarts (8 liters)
FINISH Stainless steel

● A single dishwasher with nine wash
● programs, this model also features a
  child lock and energy-saving programs.

DIMENSIONS H16 x W23'/₂ x D22'/₂
(H409 x W595 x D570)
WATER CONSUMPTION 8 quarts (8 liters)
FINISH Stainless steel / Black

● This model features nine wash programs and
● takes long-stemmed wineglasses and 12 11'/₂in
  (290mm) dinner plates.

TRADITIONAL

ABOVE Choose a dishwasher with adjustable racks for maximum usability: you will want to clean everything from large platters to fine stemware. Fit a custom door to hide the appliance in a country kitchen, if you prefer.

CONTEMPORARY

LEFT Dishdrawers offer flexibility: it is possible to wash small loads using only one drawer. This allows you to keep plates and cutlery clean, and is still energy efficient.

appliances / stove tops

DIMENSIONS
H6$^7/_8$ x W36 x D21
(H174 x W914 x D533)
BURNERS 5
FINISH White / Black/
Stainless steel / Bisque

● Gas stove top that can
● be installed over an under-
counter oven. Choose the
bisque option for a country-
style kitchen.

DIMENSIONS
H7$^1/_4$ x W30 x D21$^1/_2$
(H184 X W762 x D545)
BURNERS 5
FINISH Black / White

● Gas stove top with sealed
● burners built into glass and
ceramic surface. Includes one
ultrahigh burner and one
low burner for simmering.

DIMENSIONS
H3 x W36 x D21$^1/_2$
(H76 x W914 x D546)
BURNERS 5
FINISH Stainless steel

● Featuring three-piece cast-
● iron burners and a wok
burner, this gas stove top
has electronic ignition and
flame failure protection.

DIMENSIONS
H7$^3/_4$ x W29$^1/_2$ x D21$^1/_2$
(H196 x W749 x D545
BURNERS 4
FINISH Black / White /
Stainless steel

● With four sealed gas
● burners, this can be fitted
over an under-counter oven
on the countertop.

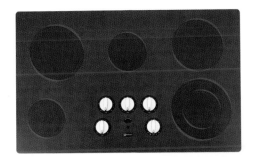

DIMENSIONS
H3³/₈ x W36 x D19³/₄
(H79 x W914 x D501)
BURNERS 5
FINISH Black / White /
Stainless steel

● An electric stove top with
five fast-heating burners,
with variable settings to
suit several pan sizes.

DIMENSIONS
H4¹/₄ x W34¹/₂ x D20³/₈
(H108 x W879 x 519)
BURNERS 5
FINISH Black / Stainless
steel

● With five burners, including
one extra high and one
extra low, this also has a
warming element to keep
food hot.

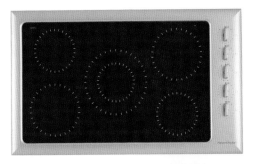

DIMENSIONS
H3 x W36 x D21¹/₂
(H 81 x W914 x D546)
BURNERS 4
FINISH Stainless steel

● A ceramic stove top with
individual hot surface
indicators and four element
sizes for maximum versatility.

DIMENSIONS
H4¹/₈ x W35¹/₄ x D21¹/₂
(H99 x W895 x D546)
BURNERS 5
FINISH Black / White /
Stainless steel

● A stove top featuring one
dual- and one triple-control
element, this also has a
quick-start element.

appliances / cast-iron ranges

DIMENSIONS H35³/₈ x W35¹/₂ x D27⁵/₈ (H898 x W900 x D700)
CAPACITY Multifunction 2.2 cu ft (62 liters), convection 1.8 cu ft (51 liters), broiler 0.5 cu ft (14 liters)
FINISH Enameled cast iron

● A cast-iron range with three ovens, five gas burners, and a broiler.

DIMENSIONS H33¹/₂ x W58⁵/₈ x D26³/₄ (H850 x W1,488 x D678)
CAPACITY Roasting 1.5 cu ft (42 liters), baking 1.5 cu ft (42 liters), simmering 1.5 cu ft (42 liters), warming 1.5 cu ft (42 l)
FINISH Enameled cast iron

● This model has four ovens, in addition to warming, boiling, and simmering plates.

DIMENSIONS H37⁷/₈ x W38³/₄ x D24¹/₂ (H962 x W982 x D621)
CAPACITY Roasting 1.2 cu ft (34 liters); baking 1.1 cu ft (31 liters), simmering 1.2 cu ft (34 liters), broiling 1.0 cu ft(28 l)
FINISH Enameled cast iron

● Range featuring six gas burners and four electric ovens, with a separate ceramic broiler.

DIMENSIONS H33¹/₂ x W58³/₄ x D26³/₄ (H850 x W1,488 x D678)
CAPACITY Roasting 1.2 cu ft (34 liters); baking 1.1 cu ft (31 liters), simmering 1.2 cu ft (34 liters), broiling 1.0 cu ft (28 l)
FINISH Enameled cast iron

● Range featuring four radiant-heat ovens, two hot plates, warming plate, and optional gas stove top.

DIMENSIONS H35⁷/₈ x W38¹/₂ x D24¹/₂ (H911 x W977 x D621)
CAPACITY Roasting 1.2 cu ft (34 liters), baking 1.1 cu ft (31 liters), simmering 1.2 cu ft (34 liters), broiling 1.0 cu ft (28 l)
FINISH Enameled cast iron

● Range with four ovens and six gas burners, including a wok and an ultra-rapid burner.

DIMENSIONS H35³/₄ x W35¹/₂ x D25¹/₂ (H908 x W901 x D647)
CAPACITY Roasting/baking 1.5 cu ft (42 liters), simmering/warming 1.5 cu ft (42 l)
FINISH Enameled cast iron

● This model has two ovens and a stove top that can accommodate five saucepans. One gas burner is designed to heat quickly.

DIMENSIONS H35³/₈ x W35¹/₄ x D25⁵/₈ (H898 x W895 x D650)
CAPACITY 4.5 cu ft (127 liters)
FINISH Enameled cast iron

● This dual-fuel (natural or propane gas and electric) model has five independent burners and comes in a choice of five colorways.

DIMENSIONS H33¹/₂ x W38⁷/₈ x D26⁵/₈ (H850 x W987 x D650)
CAPACITY Roasting 1.5 cu ft (42 l), baking 1.5 cu ft (42 l), simmering 1.5 cu ft (42 l)
FINISH Enameled cast iron

● This model—with three ovens, and simmering and boiling plates—can be left on to warm the kitchen in traditional fashion.

appliances / ranges

DIMENSIONS
H47³/₈ x W29⁷/₈ x D29
(H1,201 x W759 x D737)
CAPACITY
5.22 cu ft (148 liters)
FINISH Stainless steel

● Self-cleaning gas oven and
stove top.

DIMENSIONS
H47³/₈ x W29⁷/₈ x D29
H1,201 x W759 x D737)
CAPACITY
5.22 cu ft (148 liters)
FINISH White

● Self-cleaning four-burner
gas oven and stove top.

DIMENSIONS
H47³/₈ x W29⁷/₈ x D26⁵/₈
(H1,201 x W759 x D675)
CAPACITY
5.22 cu ft (148 liters)
FINISH Black / White /
Stainless steel / Bisque

● Freestanding range.

DIMENSIONS H36 x W30 x D29
(H914 x W762 x D737)
CAPACITY 4.2 cu ft (119 liters)
FINISH Stainless steel

● With four burners, this model also features
a broiler.

DIMENSIONS H36 x W35⁷/₈ x D29
(H914 x W911 x D737)
CAPACITY 5.3 cu ft (150 liters)
FINISH Stainless steel

● A dual-fuel range with six burners, this model
is self-cleaning.

DIMENSIONS
H46³/₄ x W29⁷/₈ x D26¹/₈
(H1,186 x W759 x D663)
CAPACITY
5.22 cu ft (148 liters)
FINISH Black / White /
Stainless steel

● Freestanding range.

DIMENSIONS
H36 x W30 x D26¹/₄
(H914 x W762 x D666)
CAPACITY
4.5 cu ft (127 liters)
FINISH Black / White /
Stainless steel / Bisque

● Freestanding range.

DIMENSIONS
H36 x W29⁷/₈ x D26¹/₄
(H914 x W759 x D666)
CAPACITY
4.5 cu ft (127 liters)
FINISH Black / White /
Stainless steel

● Freestanding range.

DIMENSIONS
H35¹/₂ x W48³/₄ x D24 (H900 x W1,216 x D610)
CAPACITY
Both ovens 2.12 cu ft (60 liters)
FINISH Stainless steel

● Self-cleaning oven with eight cooking modes, skillet
and wok burners, and internal halogen lights.

DIMENSIONS
H46³/₄ x W29⁷/₈ x D27¹/₄
(H1186 x W749 x D692)
CAPACITY
Total 5.2 cu ft (147 liters)
FINISH Stainless steel

● Free-standing range.

appliances / single ovens

DIMENSIONS H28¹/₄ x W29³/₄ x D24¹/₂
(H717 x W755 x D622)
CAPACITY 5.22 cu ft (148 liters)
FINISH Black / White / Stainless steel /
Bisque

● Self-cleaning electric oven with glass
● front, keep-warm facility, and super-sized
oven window.

DIMENSIONS H28¹/₄ x W29³/₄ x D24¹/₂
(H717 x W755 x D622)
CAPACITY 5.22 cu ft (148 liters)
FINISH Black / White / Stainless steel /
Bisque

● Self-cleaning electric oven with supersized oven
● window, glass front, and keep-warm facility.

DIMENSIONS H28¹/₄ x W29³/₄ x D24¹/₂
(H717 x W755 x D622)
CAPACITY 5.22 cu ft (148 liters)
FINISH Black / White / Stainless steel /
Bisque

● Electric convection oven with super-sized
● window, glass front, keep-warm facility, and
electronic clock with timer.

DIMENSIONS H27 x W29³/₄ x D22³/₈
(H688 x W757 x D570)
CAPACITY 3.56 cu ft (101 liters)
FINISH Stainless steel

● Offering 10 cooking modes, this model also
features a three-piece grill system and three
oven shelves. The control pad can be locked.

DIMENSIONS H28¹/₄ x W29³/₄ x D24¹/₂
(H717 x W755 x D622)
CAPACITY 4.5 cu ft (127 liters)
FINISH Black / White / Stainless steel

- Easy-to-use convection oven with a third
- element and fan to keep oven temperature consistent, and four oven racks for extra flexibility and ease of use.

DIMENSIONS H23¹/₂ x W21⁵/₈ x D21¹/₂
(H597 x W550 x D545)
CAPACITY 1.8 cu ft (51 liters)
FINISH Black / White / Stainless steel

- With seven separate oven functions, this single oven also has a variable grill and triple-glazed door.

DIMENSIONS H28¹/₄ x W29³/₄ x D24¹/₂
(H717 x W755 x D622)
CAPACITY 4.5 cu ft (127 liters)
FINISH Black / White / Stainless steel

- With automatic door lock and programmable cook time and temperature settings, this self-cleaning single oven also features an easy-clean control panel.

DIMENSIONS H29¹/₂ x W29³/₄ x D28¹/₈
(H749 x W757 x D752)
CAPACITY 4 cu ft (113 liters)
FINISH Stainless steel

- Multimode convection oven delivers the correct temperature and cooking time for different types of food.

appliances / double ovens

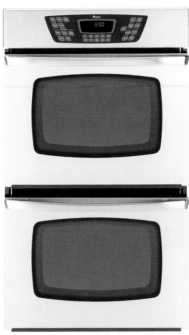

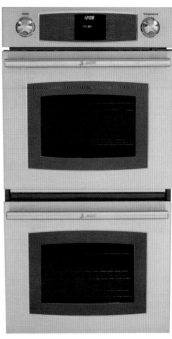

DIMENSIONS H50¹/₄ x W29³/₄ x D24¹/₂
(H1,276 x W757 x D622)
CAPACITY Total 5.2 cu ft (148 liters)
FINISH Stainless steel / Black / White

● **TOP LEFT** Double wall oven with pre-
● programmable settings.

DIMENSIONS H52¹/₄ x W26³/₄ x D24³/₄
(H1,327 x W678 x D628)
CAPACITY Each oven 3.6 cu ft (102 liters)
FINISH Black / White / Stainless steel

● **ABOVE** Double convection oven with bake
● and broil facilities.

DIMENSIONS H48¹/₂ x W29³/₄ x D22¹/₂
(H1,230 x W757 x D570)
CAPACITY Each oven 3.67 cu ft (104 liters)
FINISH Stainless steel / White

● **LEFT** With 10 cooking modes, this oven is self-
● cleaning and has a keypad lock.

DIMENSIONS H52¹/₄ x W29³/₄ x D28¹/₈
(H1,327 x W755 x D714)
CAPACITY Total 4 cu ft (113 liters)
FINISH Stainless steel

● **LEFT** A double electric wall oven with six
● convection settings for precise cooking.

DIMENSIONS H42³/₈ x W23³/₈ x D21¹/₈
(H1,077 x W595 x D562)
CAPACITY Each oven 2.82 cu ft (80 liters)
FINISH Stainless steel / White

● **BOTTOM LEFT** With eight cooking modes,
● this oven has a control pad lock, is self-
cleaning, and also features a pizza stone.

DIMENSIONS H52⁷/₈ x W29³/₄ x D27¹/₂
(H1,342 x W755 x D699)
CAPACITY 4 cu ft (113 liters)
FINISH Black / White / Stainless steel

● **BELOW** A double electric wall oven and
● microwave combination.

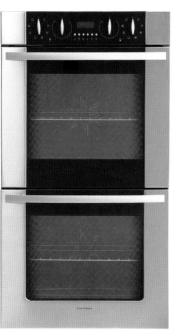

appliances / ranges and stove tops

CONTEMPORARY

ABOVE In this cool space, all surfaces, equipment, and appliances are black, white, or stainless steel. The choice of a wall-mounted double oven does not compromise the purity of the look.

TRADITIONAL

LEFT A practical gas stove top in stainless steel blends almost imperceptibly into the speckled granite countertop that sets the tone in this classic kitchen.

COUNTRY

BELOW Put together with considerable stylistic flair, this witty mix of checkerboard floor, curly metal chairs, large storage units, and cast-iron range in bright blue defines the country look.

appliances / microwave ovens

Useful and practical, a microwave has become an essential appliance in most kitchens. It is ideal for cooking in a hurry or heating the occasional precooked meal, and useful for families who find it difficult to sit down to eat at the same time. Some models feature a grill or toaster function, which saves counter space, and most models have a detrost function.

COUNTRY

LEFT Regardless of kitchen style most people want a microwave. You could hide it behind a custom door if it does not fit your overall style, or choose a neutral color to fit any space.

CONTEMPORARY

BELOW Stainless steel is usually a good choice for large, contemporary spaces. Choose white in a traditional kichen. Siting a microwave at eye level frees up counter space.

chapter **three**

This chapter presents a visual catalog of the enormous range of possibilities that exist when it comes to choosing your kitchen cabinets. The material is divided between wood and laminates, with options in dark, medium, light, and stained woods, and laminates in a range of colors. On one half of each double-page spread wood or laminate finishes are teamed with ideas for counters and tile work; on the other half, wooden doors are shown with a range of different handle options. Interspersed with these catalog pages are inspirational photographs of real kitchens in several different styles. Look through these pages to get a good feel for what you might like in your own kitchen, then look at the specific combinations as you start to fine-tune your ideas.

cabinets / general considerations

The range of cabinets is enormous. The most expensive option is to have your cabinets custom made to fit your precise needs. Alternatively, you can buy stock units off-the-shelf or via the Internet. These cabinets are available in standard sizes, although many ranges have half-units, or end-of-run fillers to create a totally filled look. If you are on a tight budget, one of your options is not to invest in a complete set of new cabinets, but simply to replace the doors of your existing ones: this can give you a new-look kitchen at a fraction of the cost of starting over.

wooden doors
Wood is probably the most common material for cabinet doors. Among the lighter woods are pine, light oak, and maple. Dark oak, hickory, and cherry are the most common darker woods, and alder is becoming increasingly popular. Many woods are treated in some way to bring out the beauty of

TRADITIONAL	SHAKER
■ Rich and deep, cherry wood mellows as it ages, and is a popular choice for both traditional and more formal kitchens.	■ Traditionally Shaker furniture was made from maple, birch, chestnut, and pine, so choose these woods if authenticity is important.
■ Modern Thermofoils can have the appearance of painted wood, so consider these, too, in making your final choice.	■ For Shaker-style cabinets, consider function, practicality, and durability above all other factors.
■ Consider a range hood to match the lines of the cupboards and create a focal point in the kitchen.	■ Shaker kitchens had a peg rail around the walls on which chairs, stools, clothing, and tools could be stored to facilitate floor cleaning. Fix a miniature version above the countertop to hold often-used utensils and equipment.
■ Invest time and—if your budget permits—money in neat, stylish drawer pulls. Try traditional brass, glass, or ceramic designs, or look for inexpensive, but good-looking, steel ones.	■ Doors and drawers are usually flush in this style, with no molding. Lines should be uncluttered but graceful, not hard edged in the modern way.
■ Inset and lipped doors are more suitable for traditional schemes than plain ones.	■ Handles were usually turned knobs; this is still an appealing look. You could also choose metallic handles in simple shapes.

the grain and the subtle variations in color. Wooden cabinet doors can also be painted or color washed. This is a good way to disguise cheaper woods, and allows you to personalize your kitchen. Choose a pale or medium tone, rather than a dark, one, both to enhance the feeling of space and to avoid camouflaging dirt and smudges.

If you have a lot of cupboards, consider buying some doors with glazed fronts, or fix open shelving to break up the uniform look.

your other options
Durable and easy to clean, laminates are plastic or polyester surfaces used to cover a core of particleboard or MDF (medium-density fiberboard). MDF is a popular choice for laminating because of its stability. Melamine is a common surface, as are Thermofoils: these are flexible vinyls that are good looking and easy to clean. Quality laminates come in almost as many colors as paint, so whatever your style and color preferences, you are likely to find something that works in your space.

CONTEMPORARY	COUNTRY
■ Thermofoil, plastic, and stainless steel are good choices for both cupboards and counters.	■ Most woods work well in a country kitchen. Use lighter woods such as pine or oak if the space is small; a larger area can take darker shades.
■ Use bright, clear color for a fresh, modern look. To reduce visual clutter in a small space, choose the same strong tone for the cabinets and walls.	■ Consider having fewer cupboards for storage and opting instead for an old-fashioned hutch to hold china and stemware.
■ Industrial materials such as aluminum or plastic—in sheet or tile form—are a good choice for splashboards.	■ To enhance the warmth and coziness of a country kitchen, bring out the warmth of real wood by leaving its natural color and using a matte varnish or a giving it a treatment with furniture wax.
■ The choice of handles is enormous in this style of kitchen: consider glass, steel, nickel, and plastic as your starting points.	■ Antique door furniture such as hinges and latches can work well in country kitchens.
■ Avoid recessed or molded doors on cabinets: clean lines work better in contemporary designs.	■ Bead-board door styles often prove effective in this type of kitchen: these have grooved vertical channels, and are usually available in wood or white finishes.

dark wood / combinations

TRADITIONAL

SHAKER

CONTEMPORARY

COUNTRY

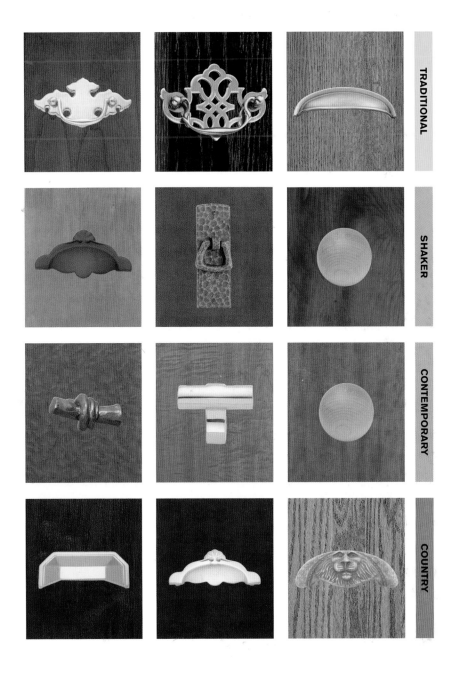

TRADITIONAL

SHAKER

CONTEMPORARY

COUNTRY

dark wood / combinations

TRADITIONAL

SHAKER

CONTEMPORARY

COUNTRY

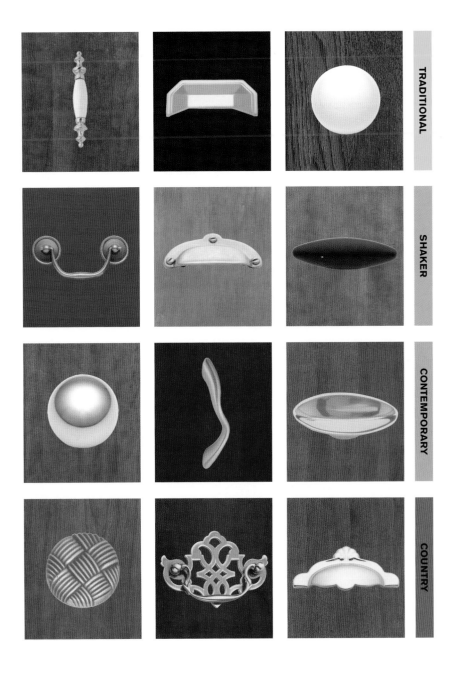

TRADITIONAL

SHAKER

CONTEMPORARY

COUNTRY

dark wood / combinations

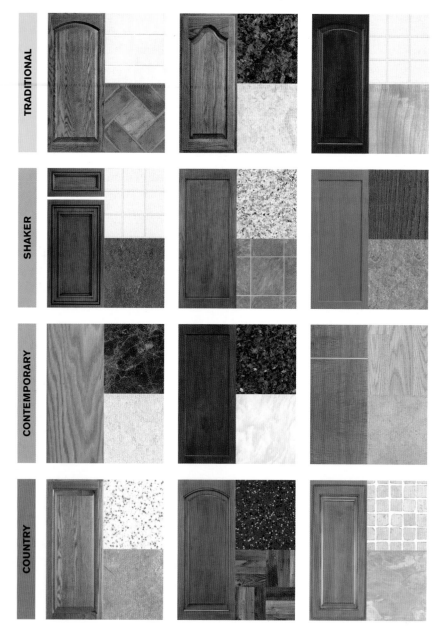

TRADITIONAL

SHAKER

CONTEMPORARY

COUNTRY

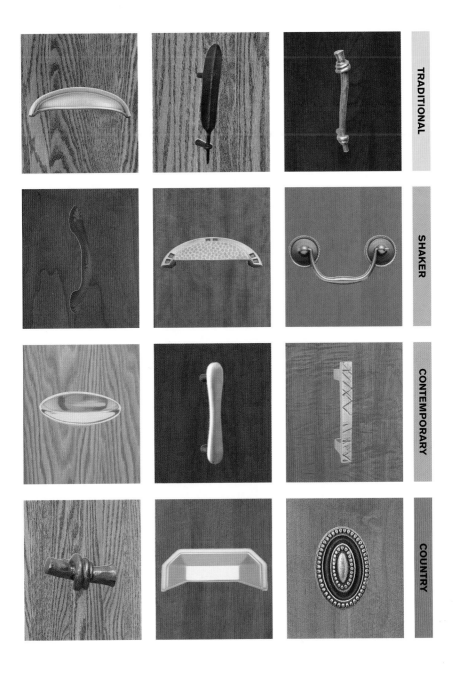

TRADITIONAL

SHAKER

CONTEMPORARY

COUNTRY

dark wood / combinations

TRADITIONAL

SHAKER

CONTEMPORARY

COUNTRY

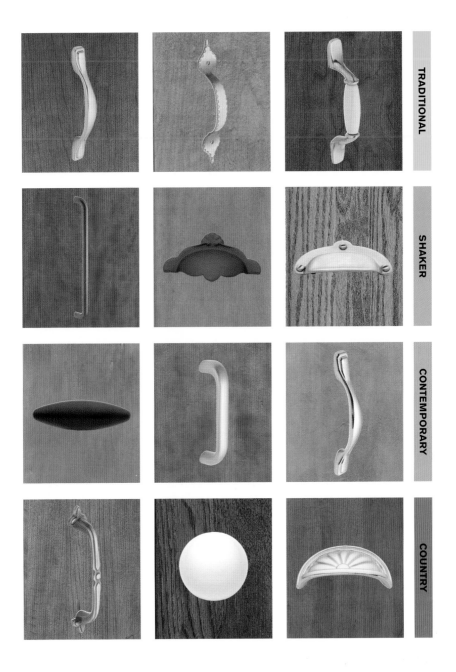

TRADITIONAL

SHAKER

CONTEMPORARY

COUNTRY

style themes / dark wood

COUNTRY

ABOVE Break up an expanse of dark wood, as in this country-style kitchen, with a painted hutch to fit the style. The island in the same dark wood as the cabinets adds unity to the look.

CONTEMPORARY

LEFT The warm glow of cherry lends itself to clean-lined modern schemes as well as cozy period ones. These simple, elegant cabinets offer the best of both looks.

CONTEMPORARY

BELOW When your cabinets are solid cherry with a highly figured grain that takes center stage, keep the details low key.

style themes / dark wood

COUNTRY

OPPOSITE To set off the rich tones of alder cabinets and a maple island unit, combine them with pale ceramic tiles and an impressive expanse of mottled marble.

TRADITIONAL

LEFT Create a rich, period atmosphere by setting off framed cherry cabinets with soft-hued walls, traditional tiles, a stone floor, and carefully chosen tableware, equipment, and accessories.

CONTEMPORARY

BELOW The sleek lines of frameless maple cabinets blend beautifully with stainless steel appliances, accessories, and detailing.

medium wood / combinations

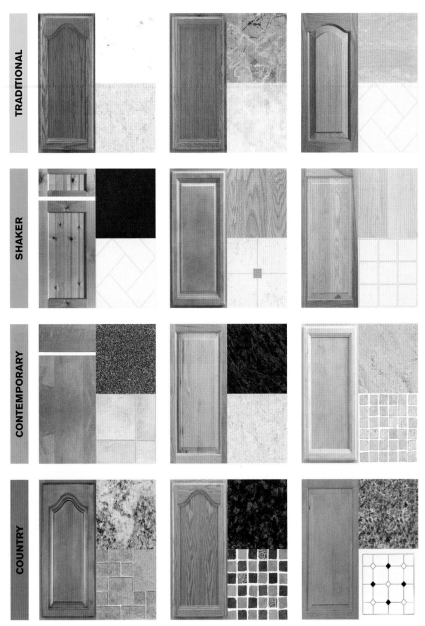

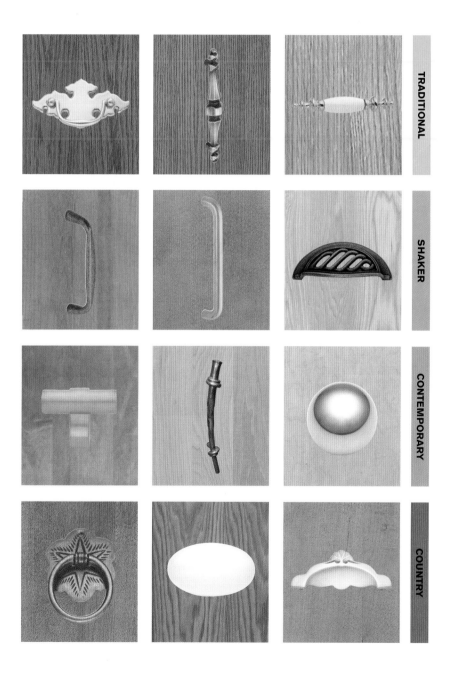

TRADITIONAL

SHAKER

CONTEMPORARY

COUNTRY

medium wood / combinations

TRADITIONAL

SHAKER

CONTEMPORARY

COUNTRY

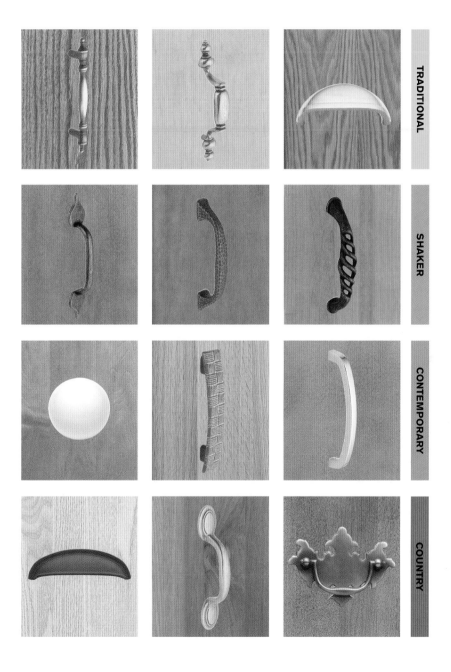

medium wood / combinations

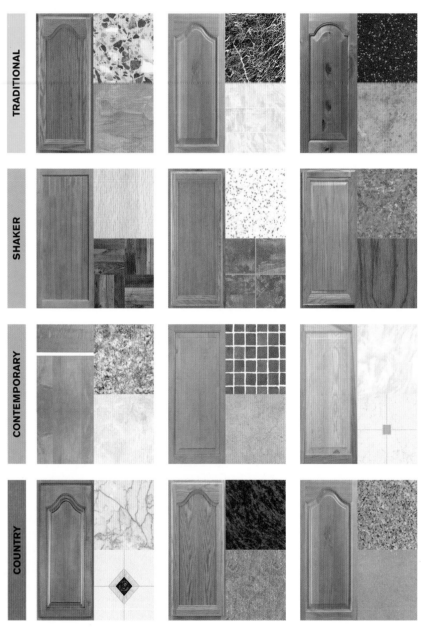

TRADITIONAL

SHAKER

CONTEMPORARY

COUNTRY

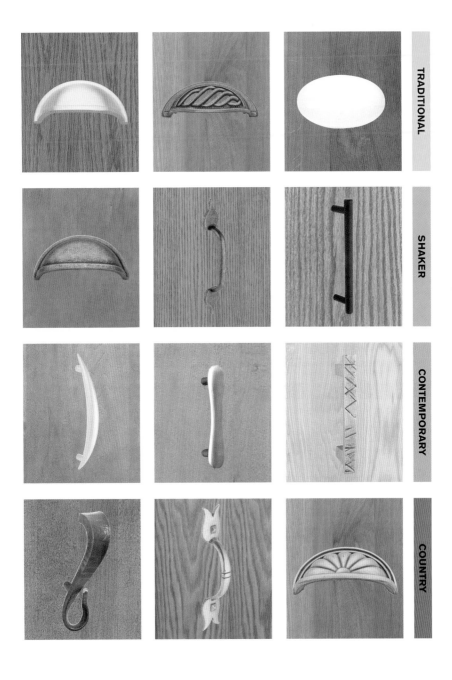

TRADITIONAL

SHAKER

CONTEMPORARY

COUNTRY

style themes / medium wood

TRADITIONAL

ABOVE Team light maple cabinets with cool blue surfaces, textural tiles, and touches of stainless steel for a look that is contemporary with a soft edge. Here, the drawer pulls add a retro touch.

SHAKER

LEFT To make an island unit less obtrusive, choose a finish that tones with the floor; this unit is maple. As well as extra work space, island units provide lots of additional storage capacity.

TRADITIONAL

BELOW In this maple kitchen old-fashioned craftsmanship maximizes storage without compromising style.

style themes / medium wood

TRADITIONAL

ABOVE To get a totally coordinated look, choose finely crafted wood (like this natural alder) for your cabinets, and for matching panels that will disguise your appliances.

COUNTRY

RIGHT Medium woods such as maple and hickory take on a warm patina as they age. In this country kitchen, white countertops contribute to the homey look.

COUNTRY

ABOVE Many traditional-style ranges are available in several different colors, and look good with most medium wood cabinets. The wall tiles add a modern touch to this kitchen.

light wood / combinations

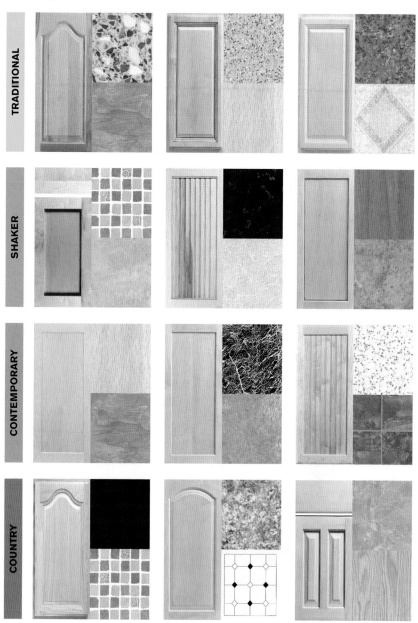

TRADITIONAL

SHAKER

CONTEMPORARY

COUNTRY

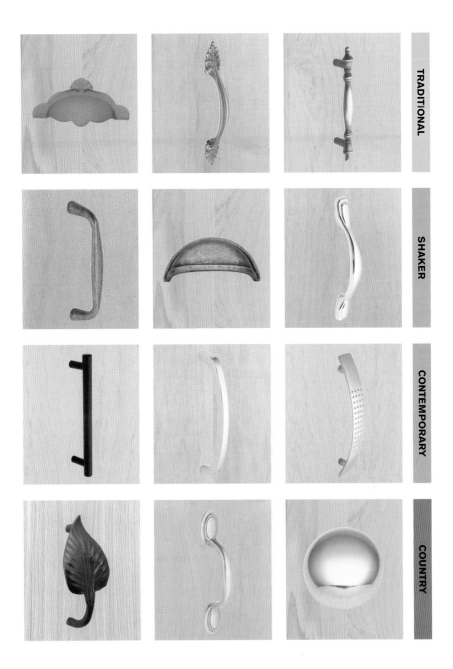

TRADITIONAL

SHAKER

CONTEMPORARY

COUNTRY

light wood / combinations

TRADITIONAL

SHAKER

CONTEMPORARY

COUNTRY

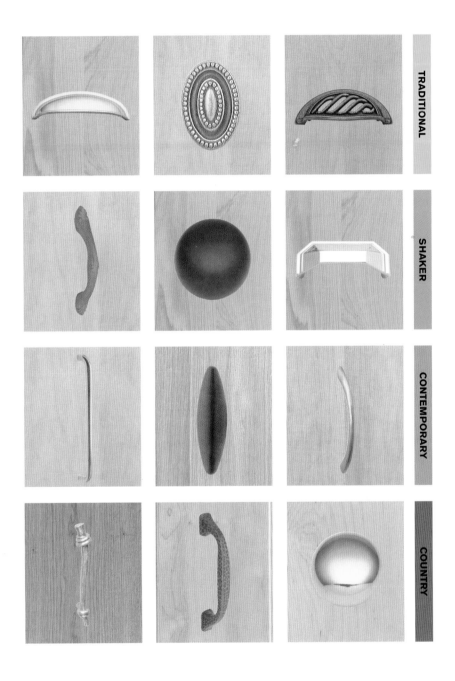

TRADITIONAL

SHAKER

CONTEMPORARY

COUNTRY

light wood / combinations

TRADITIONAL

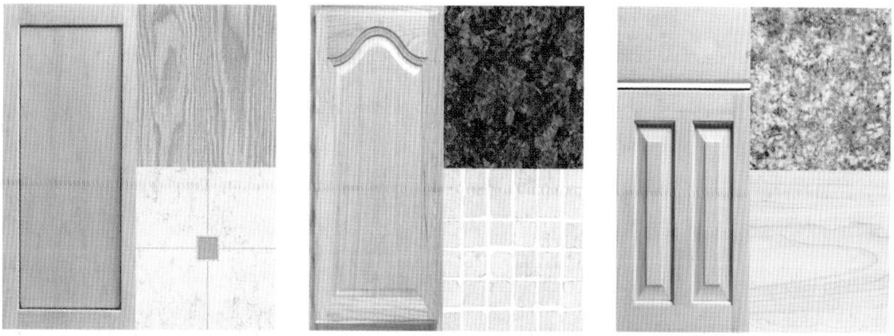

SHAKER

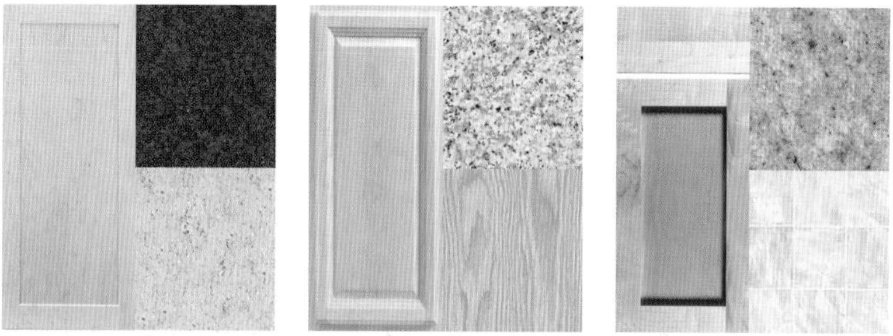

CONTEMPORARY

COUNTRY

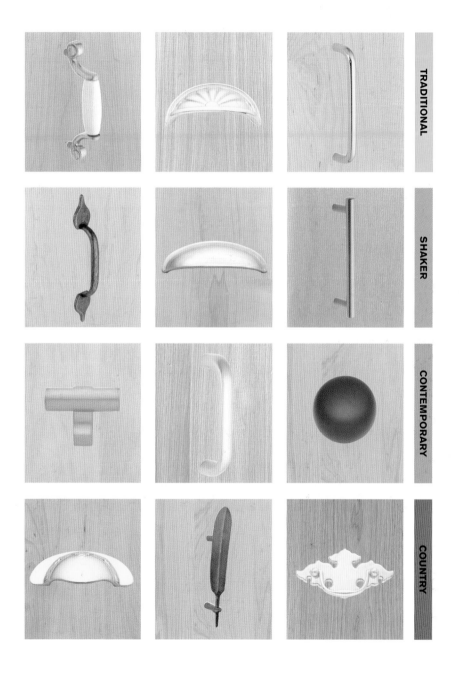

TRADITIONAL

SHAKER

CONTEMPORARY

COUNTRY

style themes / light wood

ABOVE Pale wooden cabinets contribute to the light and airy feeling in this kitchen, a feeling underscored by the clean lines of the white marble countertop. The plant and fruit bowl are colorful additions.

CONTEMPORARY

LEFT In this space, fussy details would be lost, so its owners rely on the huge range and the sleek expanses of wood and stainless steel for visual interest. Castors make the table easy to move.

SHAKER

BELOW When the look is simple, you can cover a whole wall in cabinets without creating visual clutter. Use hard-to-reach spaces for bulky things like baskets and platters that you don't use very often.

wood & glass / combinations

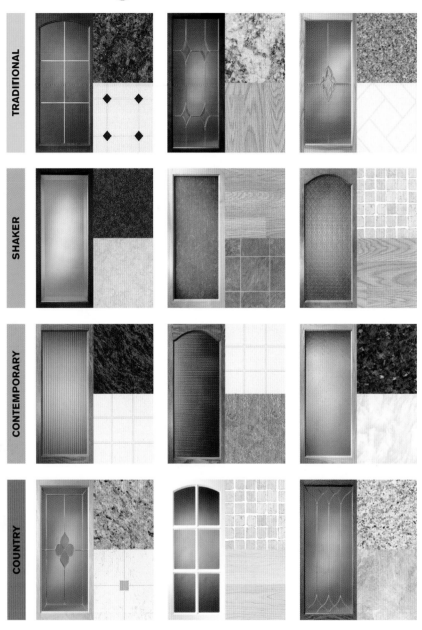

TRADITIONAL

SHAKER

CONTEMPORARY

COUNTRY

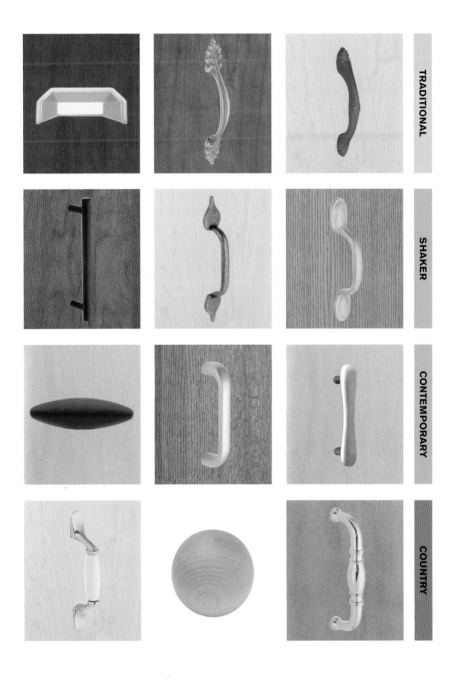

TRADITIONAL

SHAKER

CONTEMPORARY

COUNTRY

white-painted wood / combinations

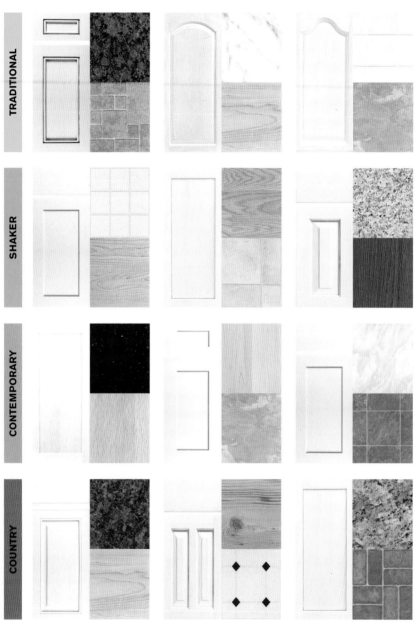

TRADITIONAL

SHAKER

CONTEMPORARY

COUNTRY

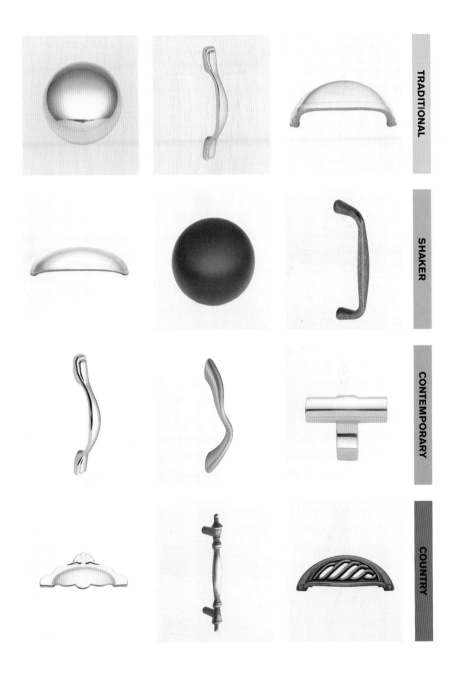

TRADITIONAL

SHAKER

CONTEMPORARY

COUNTRY

red-stained wood / combinations

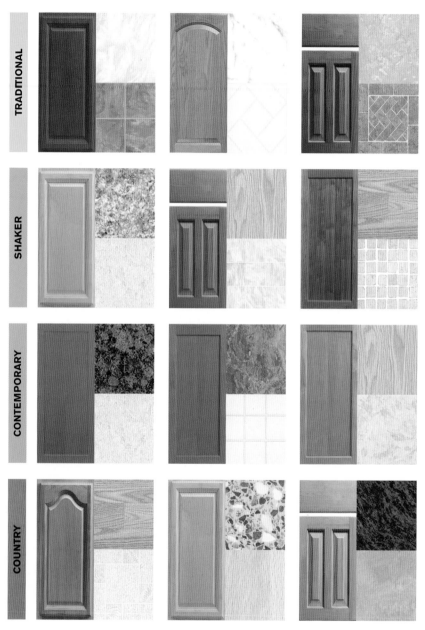

TRADITIONAL

SHAKER

CONTEMPORARY

COUNTRY

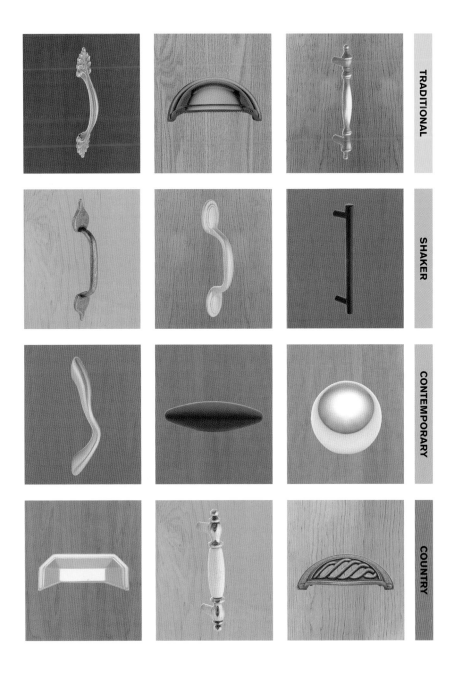

TRADITIONAL

SHAKER

CONTEMPORARY

COUNTRY

blue-stained wood / combinations

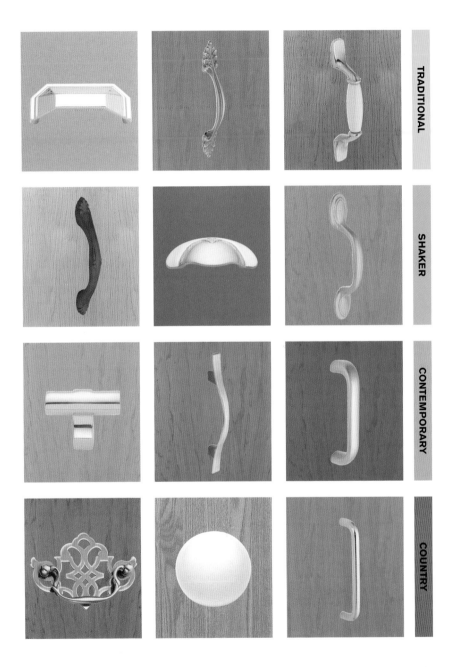

TRADITIONAL

SHAKER

CONTEMPORARY

COUNTRY

green-stained wood / combinations

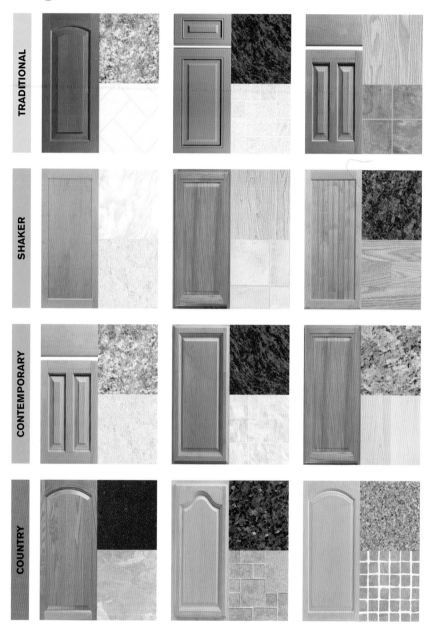

TRADITIONAL

SHAKER

CONTEMPORARY

COUNTRY

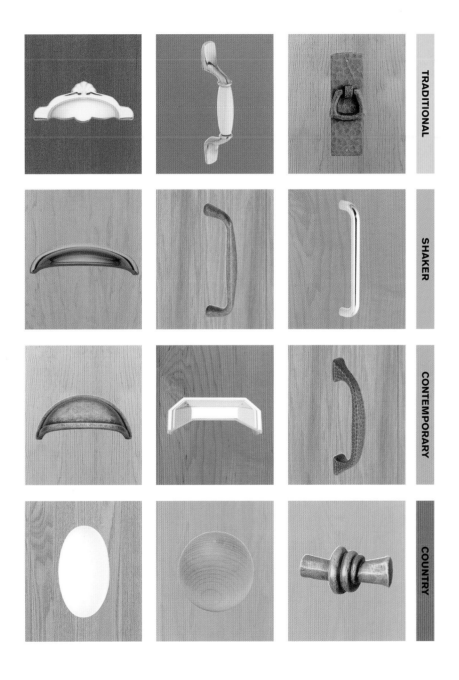

TRADITIONAL

SHAKER

CONTEMPORARY

COUNTRY

white & cream laminate / combinations

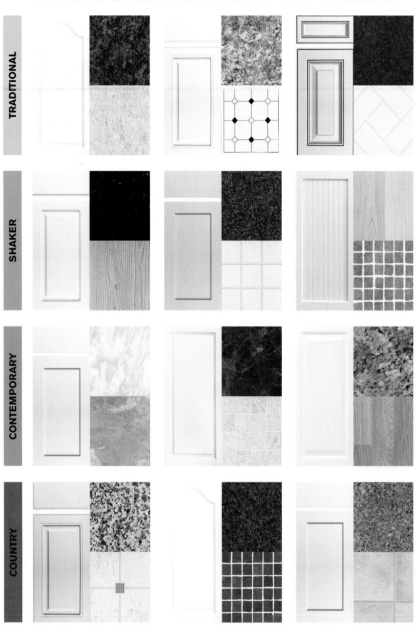

TRADITIONAL

SHAKER

CONTEMPORARY

COUNTRY

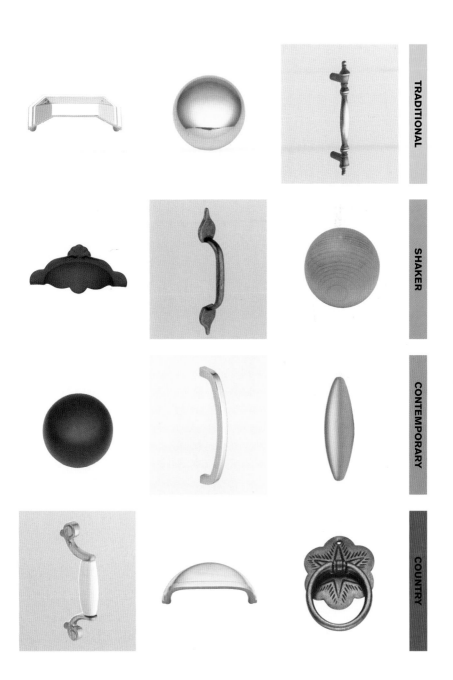

TRADITIONAL

SHAKER

CONTEMPORARY

COUNTRY

red laminate / combinations

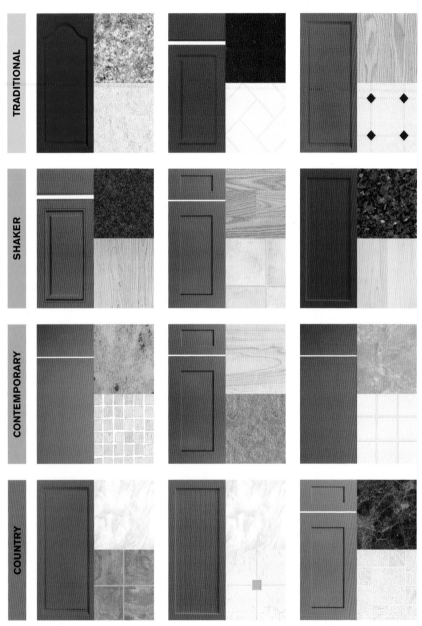

TRADITIONAL

SHAKER

CONTEMPORARY

COUNTRY

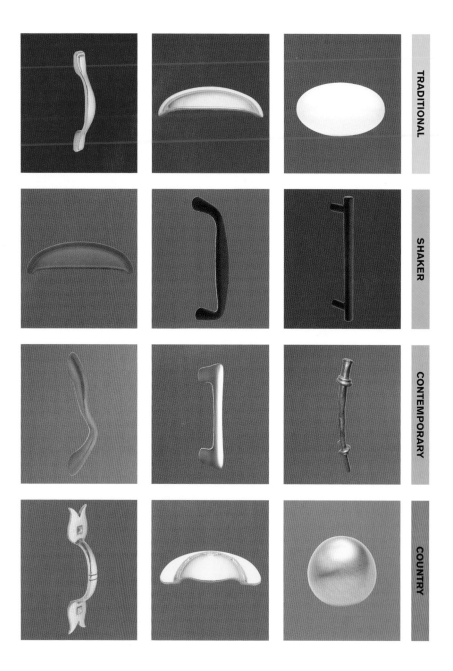

TRADITIONAL

SHAKER

CONTEMPORARY

COUNTRY

blue laminate / combinations

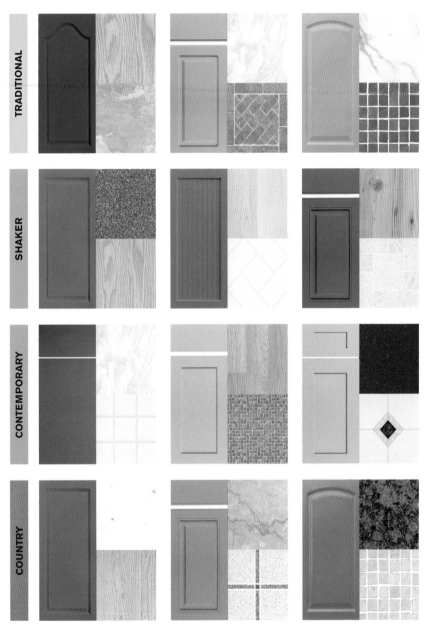

TRADITIONAL

SHAKER

CONTEMPORARY

COUNTRY

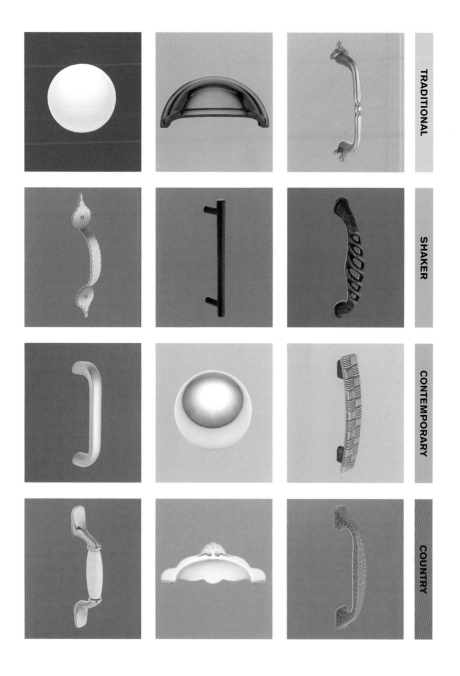

TRADITIONAL

SHAKER

CONTEMPORARY

COUNTRY

green laminate / combinations

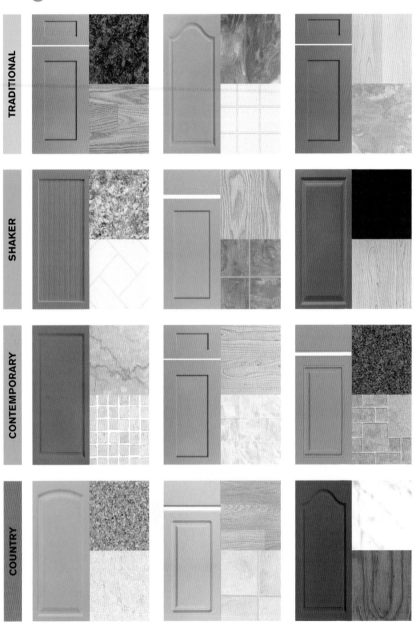

TRADITIONAL

SHAKER

CONTEMPORARY

COUNTRY

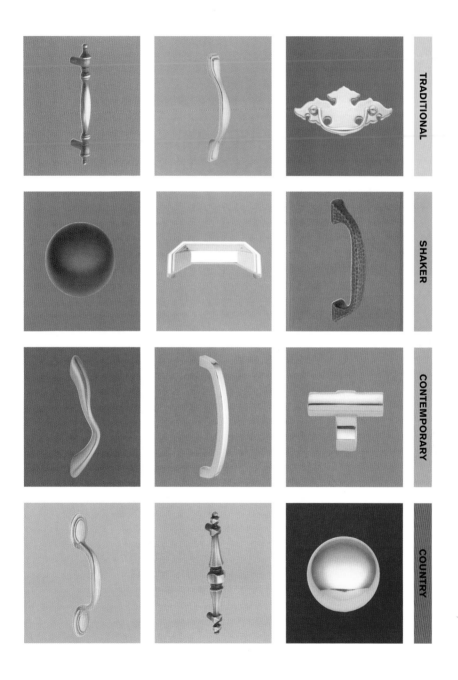

TRADITIONAL

SHAKER

CONTEMPORARY

COUNTRY

metal / combinations

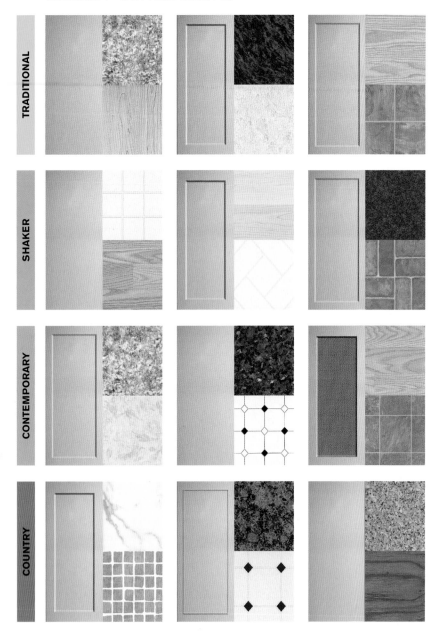

TRADITIONAL

SHAKER

CONTEMPORARY

COUNTRY

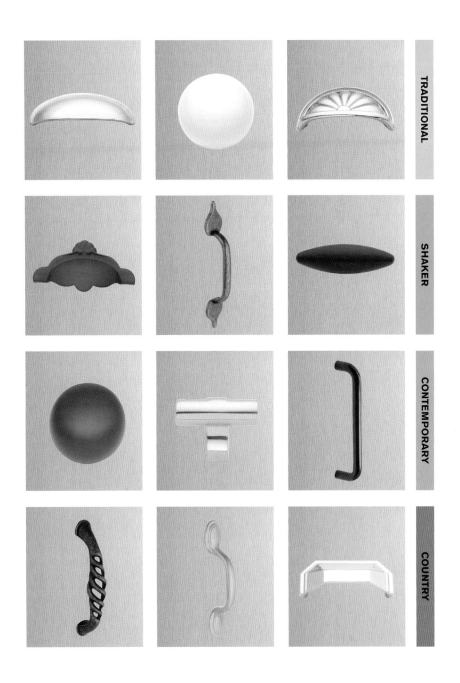

style themes / painted and laminate

SHAKER

ABOVE Create a feeling of space in a small room by giving it an all-over color treatment. Here, the simple cabinets and the faintly colonial-style wainscoting linking them have been finished with the same satiny, soft-blue paint.

CONTEMPORARY

OPPOSITE Interpreted in stark black and white, this graphic look makes use of iconic modern materials like laminate, vinyl, metal, and plastic. The huge table has a dual role as dining surface and sculpture.

COUNTRY

LEFT Give a metropolitan twist to your scheme by choosing plain laminate cabinets and setting them off with metal detailing in the form of countertops, appliances, and even light fittings like these paired white glass pendants.

style themes / laminate

CONTEMPORARY

ABOVE An all-white kitchen is a surprisingly practical choice: sleek laminate surfaces are hardwearing and easy to clean, and their purity ensures that every speck of dirt is immediately obvious.

CONTEMPORARY

LEFT Up-to-the-minute red laminate cabinets are eye-catching and practical. The surfaces are easy to wipe clean and the handles and drawer pulls are streamlined and elegant. The use of white and stainless steel lightens the overall scheme.

chapter four

Your appliances and cabinets are major considerations in your kitchen remodeling, but there are several other factors to take into account. This chapter examines some of them. Storage is a prime consideration in any kitchen, so we look at a range of options for freestanding pieces, as well as in-cupboard options. The chapter considers the different types of island units and breakfast bars, some of which may answer storage needs, too. Sinks and faucets are also looked at: these have to be chosen with care to ensure you select good-looking items that are going to last. This chapter presents a range of sinks and faucets in different styles. Finally, the chapter looks at lighting. This has to be good for safety and to effectively illuminate the many activities that take place in the kitchen.

storage / general considerations

Most people cannot have enough kitchen storage. You need storage for any foods that do not need to be refrigerated or frozen, as well as for utensils and smaller appliances that are not going to sit on the countertops. If you have the space, a walk-in pantry or larder can be ideal for both store-cupboard ingredients and small appliances. An alternative is to buy a swing-out pantry kit or a pullout drawer unit to fit into one or more of your tall cabinets. Generally, you are likely to need a mix of shelves and drawers to fit inside your base and wall units.

maximizing space

To make the most of your storage, consider what you store and how you use it. If you keep a lot of canned goods in your store cupboards, for example, buy extra shelves and set them can-height-plus-hand-clearance apart. Consider, too, the height and depth of your kitchen cabinets. In some cases

TRADITIONAL	SHAKER
■ Many manufacturers are producing storage ranges labeled "traditional" and some of these are ideal for traditional-style kitchens. Consider bread bins, and jars for frequently used ingredients such as coffee, sugar, and salt, to sit on the countertop or on open shelves.	■ Traditional Shaker kitchens had dedicated storage for almost all utensils and pieces of equipment, and more storage would be added for a new item. This practice can be emulated in a modern kitchen, with drawers for measuring cups, cookie cutters, and spices, for example, and space for oils underneath or next to the stove top.
■ Most traditional kitchens held a china cabinet for everyday items, as well as more decorative pieces. Consider this option if this is the style you are looking for.	■ Unadorned wooden shelving can be a good choice for a Shaker-style kitchen, but it is important to keep open shelves tidy—the Shaker look was uncluttered.
■ Consider your storage needs for every item of kitchen equipment, utensils, foodstuffs, linens, china, and flatware. All of these need to be accommodated and accessible.	■ Modern manufacturers of Shaker-style kitchen storage include items such as wall hutches in their ranges, and these can be a practical addition to this type of kitchen.
■ Store little-used items in the highest cupboards or deeper recesses of base units.	

pullout drawers or trays can be a more usable option than shelving in a cupboard, since they allow you to see and access contents instantly. Extra-deep drawers might fit your needs well; you could also consider deep wire baskets or drawer inserts to hold items such as flatware, plates, spices, and foil rolls, as a means of organizing your goods. In corner cupboards in particular, easy-reach or revolving carousels can be good choices: these ensure that every inch of space is used, but make access to all items easy. The alternative is a foldout shelf system that again allows access to everything stored in the cupboard.

fitted or free standing?

Storing food, equipment, and utensils behind closed doors is an option many people prefer. However, display racks for spices, plates, wine, and other items are available and, depending on your needs and overall style, these can enhance your kitchen. Most off-the-shelf kitchen lines include these items, sometimes as optional extras, occasionally as standard.

CONTEMPORARY	COUNTRY
■ Open shelving in materials such as glass and stainless steel can often prove ideal for this style of kitchen, but keep the overall look uncluttered.	■ Dressers, hutches, and lazy Susans are often appropriate for kitchens in this style. The combination of drawers and shelves may suit your storage needs better than more modern options.
■ If you choose to include some glass-fronted cabinets, remember that everything you store will be visible, so keep your choices for internal storage streamlined. Consider some solid door options if you are not confident that you will keep your cupboards tidy.	■ Consider items such as pie safes and baker's ovens—if you can find period items, the finish is likely to have gained a rich patina.
■ Wrought metal items such as baker's racks and wine racks, with or without glass shelves, are in keeping with this style.	■ A traditional butcher block may prove effective both for working at and for storage.
■ Utensil, plate, and spice drawer inserts will help to keep everything in its place.	■ Utility cabinets and pantry units in traditional woods combine modern practicality with the warmth and informality of the country kitchen.

storage / pantries

CONTEMPORARY

OPPOSITE Storage-cupboard foods come in packs and cans of all sizes, so flexible internal storage is a must. This tall larder unit can accommodate a variety of shapes and sizes.

COUNTRY

LEFT Wide shelves hidden behind streamlined doors offer good storage for equipment and utensils. The pullout baskets are ideal for smaller items and kitchen linens.

TRADITIONAL

BELOW A pantry holds all sorts of kitchen essentials. Pullout drawers and shelving ensure easy access. Door-back bins make maximum use of space.

storage / pantries

CONTEMPORARY

ABOVE For larger items of equipment that you do not want on display, choose only one or two shelves, so that it is easy to access what you need.

TRADITIONAL

OPPOSITE A pantry cupboard with a mix of drawers and shelves is a good investment. Note the door-back bins to hold smaller items.

COUNTRY

LEFT This narrow pullout unit can hold jars and bottles of different heights and makes maximum use of what could be an awkward space to fill.

storage / cupboards & drawers

CONTEMPORARY

RIGHT Swing-out drawers with wire baskets to hold cans make storage easy. Baskets are generally available in different sizes and depths to suit cans of different heights.

TRADITIONAL

BELOW In deep cabinets, pullout shelving or baskets can be a good idea, but it is important to avoid overfilling them. A heavy drawer may damage the runners.

TRADITIONAL

ABOVE A spice drawer offers a good alternative to a carousel. Storing jars in a single layer means that their contents are easy to identify, and the jars themselves can be removed and replaced easily. Drawers may be sold with or without a selection of popular culinary herbs and spices.

COUNTRY

LEFT A pullout drawer fitted into a standard or half-size base unit, with wire baskets to hold ingredients, makes good use of space. The basket is easy to wipe clean if there is leakage from a bottle or jar.

storage / cupboards & drawers

TRADITIONAL

ABOVE For china that is not going to be on display, save shelf space by buying a drawer insert. This consists of a series of pegs set at convenient intervals to hold large and small plates, as well as bowls and other pieces.

CONTEMPORARY

RIGHT A drawer dedicated to utensils with a specific slot for every piece makes preparation easy. Such inserts are usually supplied with utensils, and are not cheap, but they do keep everything neatly organized.

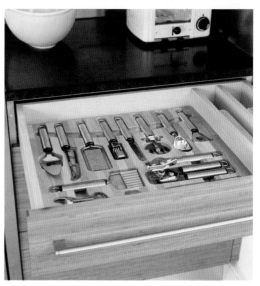

CONTEMPORARY

LEFT Wooden drawers ensure that cupboard contents do not fall out when the cupboard door is opened. This type of drawer unit also has a more appealing appearance when the door is opened: clean lines, rather than a jumble of cans and packets, contribute to the uncluttered look of a contemporary kitchen.

CONTEMPORARY

BELOW A deep drawer with an integral flatware drawer makes good use of space. Pots and pans can be stored out of sight in the bottom of the drawer, while the flatware in the top is easily accessible.

storage / cupboards & drawers

CONTEMPORARY

ABOVE A drawer unit with the appearance of a single drawer, but the storage capacity of four drawers, makes good use of space and storage options, while preserving the stream-lined look appropriate for a contemporary kitchen.

TRADITIONAL

RIGHT For fruit and vegetable storage in a traditional kitchen, opt for natural materials such as wood or wicker. These units are especially made for use in kitchens; single baskets designed to hold logs may be sold in hardware stores.

storage / cupboards & drawers

TRADITIONAL

ABOVE Double-drawer peg inserts hold plates and bowls in the lower drawer, and cups in the upper. Wooden drawer inserts to hold plates vertically are also available if that is more convenient: the plates are inserted as in a dishwasher.

CONTEMPORARY

LEFT It is possible to store glasses and cups in a drawer. To lessen the risk of breakage, drawers for this purpose are often designed with four or more separate compartments to cut down on movement when the drawer is pulled out.

CONTEMPORARY

BELOW Store aluminum pots and saucepans in pullout stainless steel drawers. This arrangement works well in an island kitchen when the stove top is located on the island with the drawers below.

storage / cupboards & drawers

COUNTRY

ABOVE For a country kitchen, choose a drawer unit with drawers of different sizes. Every item of equipment can have its place, from the cookie cutters and measuring spoons to the largest pitchers and bowls, as well as all the linens.

TRADITIONAL

RIGHT To store cookbooks in the kitchen, without risking potential grease marks and other stains, devote one or two drawers to them. This has the appearance of one drawer, but is two, to help organization.

LEFT It is convenient to store a few bottles of wine in the kitchen. Choose a narrow but deep drawer unit, with an insert to hold individual bottles. Alternatively, fit a wine rack in an awkward space, such as the end of a scenes of cabinets.

TRADITIONAL

BELOW A wooden plate rack is an attractive addition to a traditional kitchen, and breaks up a series of solid cabinets. This one incorporates small drawers designed to hold utensils and dry ingredients.

storage / plate racks

COUNTRY

ABOVE A plate rack is a useful addition, allowing you to showcase a china collection. Manufacturers of off-the-shelf lines often include such extras.

TRADITIONAL

LEFT Almost all traditional kitchens included a hutch or dresser to hold china and glass. For ease and usability, you could emulate this practice by selecting a freestanding cabinet for this purpose.

storage / bins

COUNTRY

LEFT A slide-out drawer with custom door holds the garbage can. It is also possible to fit two cans, one for garbage and one for recycling.

TRADITIONAL

BELOW On an island unit, or at the end of a breakfast bar, open shelving for often-used items or antiques, with drawers above, makes good use of space, and is both practical and decorative.

other considerations / faucets

Although you will want to buy a faucet that looks right with your sink and fits your overall kitchen style, the most important factor in selecting this kitchen essential is reliability. Faucets are time-consuming to install, so you do not want to be replacing them too often. You need to be sure you are buying a product that will withstand being turned on and off several times a day for several years, and has a hard-wearing finish that will look good, even after several years. Price is a reasonable indicator of quality, but is not guaranteed to get you the product you need.

faucet styles

There are three basic styles of faucet. In a widespread faucet, both hot and cold valves, as well as the spout, are mounted separately onto the sink. More common in bathrooms than kitchens, two-handled styles have the spout and valves set in a single base unit. In single-handled styles, hot and cold water are controlled by one knob that usually forms part of the spout. It is still possible to buy faucets in which there are individual handles to control the flow of hot and cold water, but most on the market today have valves to mix hot and cold, with the water delivered through a single spout.

DIMENSIONS H8³/₈ x W10⁷/₈ x D7⁷/₈
(H213 x W276 x D200)
FINISH Polished chrome / Blackened bronze / Stainless steel / White / Satin

● With cast brass body, and optional use
● escutcheon plate, this model features a pullout spray.

DIMENSIONS H6⁷/₈ x W10¹/₄ x D8¹/₂
(H173 x W262 x D218)
FINISH Polished chrome / Polished brass

● Single-control kitchen faucet with metal lever handle and separate spray that can be fitted through the escutcheon. Valve can be turned on and off to preferred temperature setting.

DIMENSIONS H4³/₄ x W5⁷/₈ x D6¹/₄
(H120 x W147 x D160)
FINISH Polished chrome

○ Two-handled laundry faucet, with cast brass construction and compression valving. The brass handles have color-codded red and blue hot and cold indicators.

DIMENSIONS H8¹/₂ x W2³/₄ x D9¹/₂
(H216 x W68 x D240)
FINISH Polished chrome

○ A single pull-up faucet, with a metal handle and body. Can be fitted with or without escutcheon plate.

DIMENSIONS H8¹/₈ x W10 x D9¹/₈
(H207 x W254 x D232)
FINISH Polished chrome / Bone / White and chrome / Stainless steel / White

○ Pullout spray spout with adjustable spray
● pattern for ease of use and nylon hose for quiet and smooth operation.

DIMENSIONS H7⁵/₈ x W10 x D9¹/₄
(H193 x W254 x D235)
FINISH Polished chrome / Bone / White / Velvet

○ This model has a cast brass swing spout and
● an easy-to-use metal handle. The spout is designed for extended reach into the sink.

other considerations / faucets

DIMENSIONS H13$\frac{1}{8}$ x W7$\frac{3}{4}$ x D5
(H332 x W198 x D127)
FINISH Polished chrome / Polished brass

● Two-handled center-set bar faucet, with
brass swing spout, ideal for prolonged
contact with water.

DIMENSIONS H13 x W10$\frac{7}{8}$ x D 7$\frac{1}{8}$
(H331 x W276 x D183)
FINISH Polished chrome / Blackened
bronze / Stainless steel / Polished
brass / White / Satin

● Brass body and brass swing spout, with brass
● escutcheon plate. Ceramic disk valve ensures
lifetime drip-free operation.

DIMENSIONS H12$\frac{1}{4}$ x W4 x D6
(H311 x W102 x D152)
FINISH Polished chrome / Polished brass /
White / Satin / Satin and brass /
Chrome and brass

● Center-set bar faucet with metal lever
● handles; this model is also available with
porcelain cross or lever handles.

DIMENSIONS H10 x W2$\frac{1}{8}$ x D9$\frac{1}{2}$
(H254 x W56 x D243)
FINISH Polished chrome

● Constructed from durable brass in order to
meet standards for the Safe Drinking Water
Act , this swing spout model has a separate
lever handle and hand spray.

DIMENSIONS H16¼ x W10⅞ x D9½
(H413 x W276 x D240)
FINISH Polished chrome / Blackened
bronze / Stainless steel / White /
Polished brass

● Pulldown faucet with an optional-use
escutcheon plate.

DIMENSIONS H10⅝ x W1⅞ x D8
(H270 x W48 x D205)
FINISH Polished chrome / Blackened
bronze / Polished brass / Satin

◍ Single-hole center-set bar or pantry faucet,
● with drip-free performance, smooth handle
operation, and finishes that will not tarnish
or scratch.

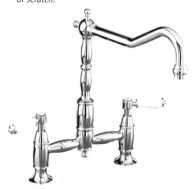

DIMENSIONS H10⅝ x W1⅞ x D8
(H270 x W48 x D205)
FINISH Polished chrome / Blackened
bronze / Polished brass / Satin

◍ Single-hole bar or pantry faucet, with smooth
● handle operation, drip-free performance, and
finish that will not tarnish or scratch.

DIMENSIONS H13⅜ x W7⅞ x D9½
(H341 x W200 x D241)
FINISH Polished chrome / Blackened
bronze / Polished brass / Satin

◍ Operated by dual porcelain lever handles,
● this top-mounted mixer faucet, also features
color-matched optional hand spray. Brass
construction for long life and smooth
drip-free operation.

other considerations / faucets

DIMENSIONS H13⅞ x W12 x D9⅜
(H352 x W301 x D238)
FINISH Polished chrome / Chrome and brass

● This model features a swivel handle, and is available with metal or porcelain lever handles and optional hand spray.

DIMENSIONS H13⅞ x W10 x D9⅜
(H352 x W254 x D238)
FINISH Polished chrome / Polished brass / White / Satin / Satin and brass / Chrome and brass

● Available with porcelain or metal cross or lever handles, this model comes with optional hand spray.

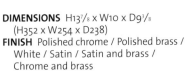

DIMENSIONS H13⅞ x W10 x D9⅜
(H352 x W254 x D238)
FINISH Polished chrome / Polished brass / White / Satin / Satin and brass / Chrome and brass

● With optional hand spray and optional
● escutcheon plate, this model is available with a choice of four handle styles.

DIMENSIONS H9¼ x W1⅞ x D6½
(H235 x W46 x D165)
FINISH Polished chrome / Stainless steel / Polished brass / Satin / Satin and brass/ Chrome and brass

● Single-hole bar or pantry faucet with cross
● handles and brass swing spout. Meets Safe Drinking Water Act requirements.

DIMENSIONS H12¹/₂ x W8 x D9
  (H317 x W203 x D229)
FINISH Polished chrome

● **TOP** A wall-mounted mixer faucet with
● scratch- and tarnish-resistant finish, this
   model is available with metal or porcelain
   lever handles.

DIMENSIONS H7³/₈ x W8 x D10⁷/₈
  (H187 x W203 x D276)
FINISH Polished chrome

● **ABOVE** Wall-mounted faucet with swing
   spout, choice of metal or porcelain lever
   handles, and integral soap dish.

other considerations / faucets & sinks

COUNTRY

ABOVE This faucet features modern materials, but retains an antique country shape in the detailing. It complements beautifully the deep sink set into a light wood countertop.

CONTEMPORARY

LEFT A high-specification and high-tech faucet, this model includes memory position valving so that the user can turn the valve on and off to a preferred temperature setting without adjusting the handle position each time.

TRADITIONAL

BELOW Stylish and practical, this is a classic model that comes with a lifetime guarantee, and is available in several finishes to suit most kitchens. The color-matched hand spray is optional.

other considerations / faucets & sinks

TRADITIONAL

ABOVE Traditional wooden cabinets, with a granite countertop, butcher's sink, and classic chrome faucet, are timeless. The porcelain handles and turned detailing are good touches.

CONTEMPORARY

LEFT Stainless steel is ideal for contemporary kitchens, hard wearing and good looking. This single sink with drainer is teamed with simple-action pull-down handles for years of easy use.

COUNTRY

BELOW A double sink is vital if you do a lot of entertaining. Team clean white styling on the sink with a chrome mixer faucet and traditional-style handles. Note that there is a hand spray for each sink.

other considerations / sinks

The kitchen sink is the most used sink in the house. Your initial choice will be the size you need. A double-bowl model is generally more adaptable, but a large single bowl will take up less counter space. You then need to decide whether the sink has to accommodate a garbage disposal unit, too, and be sure you have space for the necessary plumbing beneath the sink. Faucet style should also be considered: some sinks limit your choice of faucet to a single style; others can accommodate separate hot and cold faucets.

choice of materials

The most popular material for kitchen sinks is stainless steel. If you opt for this, you have two further things to consider. The first is the grade, or gauge, of steel: that is, how thick it is. The lower the number, the thicker the gauge. Thicker gauges wear better but are harder to install. You should also consider how well the sink absorbs sound. Especially if you wash a lot of pots and pans by hand, you do not want a sink that makes a lot of noise. It is possible to get a spray coating applied to help to reduce noise: some of these also help to keep the water temperature hotter for longer.

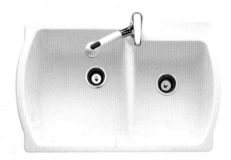

DIMENSIONS H8½ x W18 x D18
(H216 x W457 x D457)
FINISH Porcelain, 12 colors

● Single-bowl sink ideal for islands, this can be fitted with one or three faucet hole configurations. It is suitable for tile edge, self-rimming, or under-counter installation, and available in 12 colors.

DIMENSIONS H10½ x W36 x D22
(H266 x W914 x D559)
FINISH Bone / Cameo white / Glacier white porcelain

● A double-bowl sink available with single, three, and four faucet hole options. This sink is self-rimming and fits a standard 36in (914mm) base unit.

DIMENSIONS H9½ x W33 x D22
   (H241 x W838 x D559)
FINISH Porcelain, 12 colors

● **ABOVE** A double sink that can be self-
● rimming, tile edged, or fit under a counter. This
   model is available with center hole only, or
   three, four, or five faucet hole configurations.
   Several optional accessories are available, and
   the sink is available in 12 colors.

DIMENSIONS H9½ x W41½ x D22
   (H241 x W1,054 x D559)
FINISH Porcelain, 12 colors

● **BELOW** Available as a self-rimming model or
● for under-counter installation, with one
   three, four, or five faucet hole configurations,
   this three-bowl sink is available in a range of
   12 colors for maximum choice. Optional
   accessories complete the look.

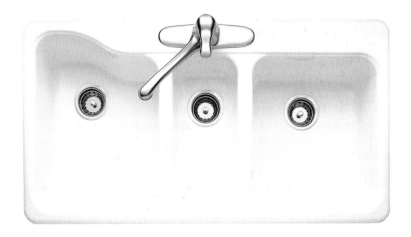

other considerations / sinks

Practical and durable, stainless steel sinks are available as single, one-and-a-half, and double-bowl, as well as square, rectangular, and circular models.

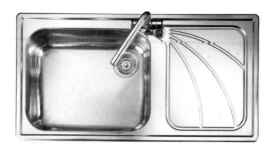

DIMENSIONS
W38 x D20(W965 x D510)
Bowl W17 x D17 x H6^{7}/$_{8}$
(W430 X D430 x H175)

● Single-bowl sink with recessed drainer, and large bowl designed to take oven trays. Available with left-hand and right-hand drainer.

DIMENSIONS
W38 x D20 (W965 x D510)
Bowls W16^{1}/$_{2}$ x D6^{7}/$_{8}$ x H5
(W420 x D175 x H130)
W6^{1}/$_{2}$ x D11^{3}/$_{4}$ x H5
(W165 x D300 x H130)

● This one-and-a-half-bowl sink with recessed draine is available with either left-hand or right-hand drainer.

DIMENSIONS
W39^{3}/$_{4}$ x D20^{1}/$_{4}$
(W1,010 x D515)
Bowl W15^{3}/$_{4}$ x D16^{1}/$_{2}$ x
H7^{1}/$_{2}$ (W400 x D420 x
H190)

● Single-bowl sink to fit flush for a hygienic appearance. Also available in one-and-a-half and double-bowl options.

DIMENSIONS
W39^{3}/$_{4}$ x D20^{1}/$_{4}$
(W1,010 x D515)
Bowls W13^{3}/$_{4}$ x D16^{1}/$_{2}$ x
H7^{1}/$_{2}$ (W350 x D420 x
H190)

● A double-bowl model with centrally located faucet, this can be fitted with a waste unit.

DIMENSIONS
W39¹/₄ x D20¹/₂
(W1,000 x D520)
Bowl diam 16¹/₂ x H7¹/₂
(420 x H189)

● A reversible model, this keyhole sink offers a good-sized bowl and good drainage area.

DIMENSIONS
W39³/₄ x D20¹/₄
(W1,010 x D515)
Bowl W15³/₄ x D16¹/₂ x
H7¹/₂ (W400 x D420 x
H190)

● Single-bowl sink with brushed-finish drainer, also available as a one-and-a-half bowl model.

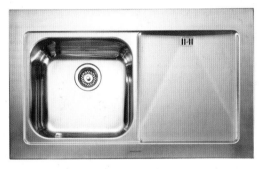

DIMENSIONS
W39³/₄ x D20¹/₄
(W1,010 x D515)
Main bowl W15³/₄ x
D16¹/₂ x H7¹/₂ (W400 x
D420 x H190)

● One-and-a-half bowl sink with a central-mounted installation hole for faucet.

DIMENSIONS
W39¹/₂ x D25³/₄
(W1,000 x D655)
Bowl W13³/₄ x D16¹/₂ x H7¹/₂
(W350 x D420 x H190)

● Single bowl model with polished finish and contrasting brushed finish drainer. Additional features include contoured splashboards.

other considerations / faucets & sinks

CONTEMPORARY

ABOVE A corner-mounted faucet can be a good-looking and practical option. The goosenecked faucet and single-action handle look stylish, and team well with the stainless steel sink.

CONTEMPORARY

RIGHT Clean lines epitomize the contemporary look, as demonstrated in this square-edged sink. The pull-up handle is echoed in the simple lines of the cabinet door handles. Note that this sink is also fitted with a hand spray.

COUNTRY

LEFT On an island unit, space may be limited, but you still want the flexibility of washing vegetables and hands. Choose a small square top-mounted sink and team it with an easy-action lift-up-handle faucet.

TRADITIONAL

BELOW Where there is space for separate hot and cold faucets, you may prefer to install them. Traditional handles may suit your kitchen, or easy-turn valves, as here, may be more in keeping with your overall style.

other considerations / gadgets

There is a huge range of gadgets: some essential and others of limited use to most people. How you use the kitchen and how much space you have are going to have an impact on what you choose to include. A warming drawer for plates and foods can be a good option for anyone who does a lot of entertaining, for example. Anything that fits an awkward space, such as a narrow refrigerator or dishwasher, can be a good addition. If you prefer to keep some wine in the kitchen, a wine rack or cooler is useful.

When deciding whether to make room for small appliances such as coffeemakers and ice makers, consider how often you will use them before devoting counter space to them.

TRADITIONAL

BELOW A narrow, under-counter, pullout refrigerator may meet your needs for access to cold ingredients when you are preparing food. The family refrigerator can be located elsewhere.

CONTEMPORARY

ABOVE One or even more refrigerated drawers can be good choices for fresh foods, integrating into the kitchen units while keeping food cool.

COUNTRY

LEFT Refrigerated drawers make maximum use of every area of an island unit. Colored options are available from some manufacturers.

CONTEMPORARY

ABOVE A warming drawer is a modern solution to the timeless problem of keeping food warm when guests are late, and allows you to finish last-minute preparations. Choose a model with variable temperature settings and moisture control so that food texture is preserved.

CONTEMPORARY

OPPOSITE Wine chillers can be used as storage in the cellar while wines age, or in the kitchen for day-to-day needs. Choose a model with variable temperature and humidity controls for the greatest flexibility. Some models take custom cabinet doors to fit into any style.

TRADITIONAL

ABOVE A 30-bottle wine chiller may fit your needs. Choose a model with a temperature gradient to store red wine near the top and white wines at the bottom. Alternatively, opt for a model with separate temperature controls for two distinct storage areas.

CONTEMPORARY

LEFT A wine chiller that holds 100 bottles is for serious wine connoisseurs. Models are likely to have two separate temperature zones to keep reds, and whites and roses, at the right temperature.

CONTEMPORARY

ABOVE An under-counter, built-in ice maker can be a useful addition. Choose a model that filters impurities from the water before freezing. Black, white, and stainless steel options suit this style.

COUNTRY

LEFT To store wine bottles horizontally, choose a wine bar. An undercounter model may meet your needs: it is easy to incorporate into a series of units, and the wine is to hand.

CONTEMPORARY

ABOVE AND RIGHT Modern dishdrawers combine the practicality of a dishwasher with the flexibility of washing a few items by hand. These machines are energy efficient and economical to run. In addition to looking good, they are easy to integrate into most kitchen storage units.

TRADITIONAL

LEFT The aroma of fresh coffee is appealing in a home. A coffeemaker takes up space, but it may be worth it to you. Some models include a drawer for cups and saucers.

other considerations / island units

There are many advantages to an island unit. In a large kitchen it can reduce the amount of time you spend walking from workstation to workstation. A large island can be dedicated to cooking, for example, with space above and below for pots and pans, utensils, and frequently used ingredients such as oils and seasonings.

fixed or not?

Your major decision in installing an island is whether it should be fixed or movable. A fixed island can provide the focal point of the kitchen and allows at least one of the major functions, such as preparation, cooking, or dish washing, to be carried out there. A movable island is more flexible and can be ideal in a smaller kitchen where space is limited. Where one person is involved with cooking, food can be prepared or served on the island in any convenient location.

COUNTRY

BELOW Siting the stove top on an island, with space on either side for food preparation and serving, cupboard space for cookware, and drawer space for utensils, is an efficient use of space.

CONTEMPORARY

LEFT Castors make an island unit easy to move. Sliding drawers cut down on clearance space, so this is a good option for smaller kitchens.

BELOW Light wood and clean lines, with good storage, make this island suitable for a range of modern kitchens.

TRADITIONAL

BELOW This wood-topped island unit incorporates the sink and refrigerator, in addition to ample space for chopping and mixing, making food preparation very efficient.

TRADITIONAL

ABOVE White cabinets and counters and flooring in mid-toned wood used in all areas of the kitchen, including the island, create a light and airy space. Note that there are two sinks, one sited on the island.

TRADITIONAL

LEFT A hanging pendant light illuminates the island, making food preparation easy. The large working area allows more than one person to work at the same time, and there is ample storage space below.

CONTEMPORARY

BELOW Striking red cabinets add glitz to this informal kitchen. White cabinets on the island add extra storage. The black granite counter tones with the cast-iron range and adds visual continuity.

CONTEMPORARY

RIGHT AND BELOW A dual-height island, as shown in this large kitchen, allows food preparation at a convenient height, and allows regular-height dining chairs to be pulled up for eating in comfort. Siting the stove top and oven on the island means that food can be cooked, served, and consumed in a smooth logical sequence. The wooden surface of the eating area of the island tones well with the open shelving on the walls to provide visual coherence in this large and airy kitchen.

COUNTRY

BELOW Butter yellow walls and cabinets, and a blue island, make this a cheerful kitchen. The wicker baskets are a good finishing touch.

CONTEMPORARY

ABOVE In this spacious and airy, contemporary kitchen, the island is the focal point of the design, with space for all food preparation and cooking. The ventilation hood is functional and contributes to the overall success of the design scheme.

COUNTRY

RIGHT Throughout this kitchen classic maple cabinets with raised panels and applied molding are used. The island includes a second sink to facilitate food preparation.

CONTEMPORARY

ABOVE White, steel, and wood are used throughout this clean-lined contemporary kitchen. The super-deep island countertop houses both stove top and sink, and leaves plenty of room for food preparation, with ample storage beneath.

CONTEMPORARY

LEFT A sleek, streamlined look is created by this large white island. The legs contribute to the sense of airiness, while the curved door detailing echoes the round sink and adds a retro touch.

CONTEMPORARY

ABOVE Walnut cabinets create warmth in this large space. The long island with curved edge is finished in durable granite.

TRADITIONAL

RIGHT Wooden cabinets in mid tones, along with turned detailing on the island unit and glazed wall cabinet doors, contribute to the warmth and informal feel of this traditional-style kitchen.

SHAKER

LEFT Practical work surfaces, with blond wood cabinets, and a functional black cast-iron range with hood, contribute to the success of this scheme.

CONTEMPORARY

BELOW The steel detailing on the drawers of the white cabinets is echoed on the island's cabinets and in the ventilation hood. A towel rail—here in chrome—is a good addition to an island.

considerations / breakfast bars & seating

Most kitchens need an informal eating area, where breakfast can be served and children can have a snack after school. If you have an island kitchen, you could incorporate a breakfast bar, either at a high level when tall stools are the best seating option, or lower down when standard-height chairs will work. An alternative is to buy a couple of tall stools and use an area of the countertop as a space for eating.

more formal dining

If your kitchen is also your dining space, buy a table and chairs to complement the overall style and décor. Folding chairs are an option if space is limited and for occasions when guests arrive: these can be stored away when not in use.

COUNTRY

BELOW A country kitchen is often the focal point of a home. Here the long table can be used as an additional food preparation area and for children to do homework within sight of the main kitchen work areas, as well as for family dining and entertaining.

CONTEMPORARY

ABOVE A simple movable stool, with white legs to tone with the kitchen cabinets and a wooden top to match the countertop, looks very stylish.

TRADITIONAL

RIGHT A dual-height island
unit and breakfast bar is a
useful addition to the kitchen,
offering flexible use of space
for different activities to be
pursued simultaneously.

CONTEMPORARY

BELOW A gloss finish and
feature doors bring traditional
maple cabinets right up to
date. The counter provides
an informal dining space.

CONTEMPORARY

LEFT Where space is less of an issue, you have the option of a more formal dining table and chairs, for entertaining as well as for family mealtimes.

COUNTRY

BELOW An area of breakfast bar that overhangs the main island unit allows storage of stools or chairs beneath it, when they are not in use, streamlining the look and maximizing the use of space.

CONTEMPORARY

OPPOSITE A super-sized ventilation hood and recessed down lights add to the drama of this loft-style space.

CONTEMPORARY

RIGHT White walls and pale wooden cabinets, together with the glass roof, create a light and airy space.

CONTEMPORARY

BELOW High-level bar stools allow for snacks and meals while someone is working in the main part of the kitchen.

COUNTRY

ABOVE In this largely white space, with cabinets made from Thermofoil, the maple island adds a stylish touch to an eating area.

TRADITIONAL

RIGHT The traditional wooden cabinets and breakfast bar in light tones are brought up to the minute by the chairs, which create a good informal eating space.

TRADITIONAL

ABOVE Bright blue accents contribute cheery notes in this informal space. The flowers provide a visual link between the kitchen and outdoors.

lighting / general considerations

Your lighting scheme needs thought: any extra cabling must be added at the planning stages (see pp. 38–40). Once you have a supply, you can fine-tune your ideas on looks and styles. Many people opt for a mix of materials and finishes, with traditional styles and finishes for pendants and wall lights to provide ambient lighting, and more modern finishes for items like spotlights and under-counter tracks for task and accent lighting.

shelf life of lighting

With energy efficiency increasingly high on consumers' agendas, these are the factors to consider in making your choices. An incandescent light burns for around 1,000 hours, and halogens about 3,000 hours. A fluorescent burns for up to 20,000 hours, and the newer compact fluorescents—developed for places where a full-size tube would not fit, and so reliance on incandescents was necessary—for about 8,000 hours. Lights that burn for longer, while more expensive to buy initially, are more economical in the long run.

TRADITIONAL

ABOVE Bouncing light from the top of cabinets off the ceiling contributes to overall light levels; under-cabinet lights illuminate the counters.

CONTEMPORARY

LEFT Spotlights installed on the shelves cast a light up onto the pale wall. Integral task lighting in the ventilation hood means that the stove top is in good light.

CONTEMPORARY

OPPOSITE There is a good level of ambient light in this kitchen, but daylight cannot be relied on when the kitchen may be used from early morning until late at night.

lighting / style themes

CONTEMPORARY

ABOVE Small bright spots of concentrated light, with pools to flood the sink and stove top, create a stylish, but functional, look in a modern space.

SHAKER

LEFT In this functional space, ceiling spotlights give good ambient light, while under-counter spotlights and lights under the ventilator illuminate the main work areas.

COUNTRY

ABOVE Traditional-style pendants set close together in the ceiling illuminate the surface of the table, and contribute to ambient light levels without compromising the informality of the look. Accent lights in the cabinets highlight the collection of cream china.

TRADITIONAL

LEFT Ceiling spotlights contribute to overall light levels in this kitchen, while the pendants can be fitted with dimmers for atmosphere. Light from outside contributes to ambient light levels.

lighting / up lights or down lights?

TRADITIONAL	CONTEMPORARY
ABOVE A well-chosen and well-positioned up light will flood light high in a small cone-shaped area, and offer a more diffused light over a larger but shallower area.	**RIGHT** A movable down light with adjustable height above the dining or working area serves as ambient light when retracted and as task light at lower levels.

CONTEMPORARY

BELOW In this scheme lights at different levels provide both upward illumination and diffused light. These practical lights make good use of the ceiling features.

lighting / traditional pendants

DIMENSIONS H21$\frac{1}{4}$ x diam 22$\frac{3}{4}$
(H540 x diam 580)
FINISH Antique brass
WATTAGE 250W

● **BELOW** An up light with a peach-colored
● glass shade, this model is also available with
an opal glass shade.

DIMENSIONS H21$\frac{1}{4}$ x diam 22$\frac{3}{4}$
(H540 x diam 580)
FINISH Solid brass
WATTAGE 250W

● **ABOVE** An up light in solid brass with a
● hand-applied ivory and gold finish. The shade
is in scavo (etched) glass.

DIMENSIONS H18$\frac{1}{2}$ x L34$\frac{1}{2}$ x diam 12$\frac{1}{2}$
(H470 min x L876 x diam 317)
FINISH Antique brass / Glass
WATTAGE 150W max each bulb

● **BELOW** Ideal over a breakfast bar or dining
table, this billiard-room-style light has brass-
rimmed, peach-colored glass shades and
brass fittings.

DIMENSIONS H24³/₄ x diam 18
  (H630 x diam 460
FINISH Polished brass / Polished
  unlacquered brass / Antique / Light
  aluminum / Bronze
WATTAGE 60W

● **BELOW** Hand-crafted, individual replica
● Victorian hanging lamp, available in several
  different finishes to suit many kitchen styles

DIMENSIONS H12¹/₂ min x diam 15
  (H320 min x diam 380)
FINISH Antique brass / Glass
WATTAGE 150W max

● **ABOVE** A traditional down light with shade
● made from peach-colored glass, this has a
  light mahogany top piece. Works best with a
  globe-shaped bulb.

DIMENSIONS H10 x diam 41
  (H250 x diam 1,040)
FINISH Satin nickel / Glass
WATTAGE 40W each bulb

● **BELOW** Six-bulb model that is ideal for low
  ceilings, as well as over long tables or
  breakfast bars, this halogen light offers up to
  240 watts of illumination. Made in brass with
  satin nickel finish.

lighting / pendants

DIMENSIONS H22 x diam 15
(H560 x diam 380)
FINISH SAtin nickel
WATTAGE 250W max

LEFT A simple and striking up light giving
good diffused light, this model can also be
supplied with a shade made from peach-
colored glass.

DIMENSIONS H21³/₄ x diam 13
(H550 x diam 330)
FINISH Antique brass / Glass
WATTAGE 150W max

RIGHT This up light with peach-colored glass
gives a warm, diffused light. Made from brass
with an antique brass finish, it is not suitable
for low ceilings.

DIMENSIONS H28¹/₄ min x L47¹/₂
   (H720 min x L1,206)
FINISH Satin nickel / Glass
WATTAGE 150W max each bulb

● **ABOVE** With this down light featuring blue
glass shades that cast a bluish glow, most
light is reflected down. The height can be
adjusted on installation. Suitable for
breakfast bars and dining areas.

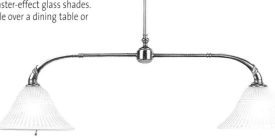

DIMENSIONS H21¹/₂ min x diam 35
   (H550 min x diam 890)
FINISH Pearlized silver
WATTAGE 60W max each bulb

● **RIGHT** A versatile light supplied with three
rod lengths to suit different needs, this
pendant has alabaster-effect glass shades.
It would be suitable over a dining table or
breakfast bar.

lighting / contemporary pendants

DIMENSIONS H65 x diam 10
(H1,650 x diam 250)
FINISH Lacquered aluminum
WATTAGE 75W max

- A good light for overall illumination, this model can be hung from a ceiling hook.

DIMENSIONS H61 max x diam 11³/₄
(H1,550 max x diam 300)
FINISH Steel / Glass
WATTAGE 75W max

- Glass globe is blown by mouth, so each one is
- unique. On this light, the hanging wire can be adjusted to allow the light to hang at the desired height.

DIMENSIONS H69 max x diam 9¹/₂
(H1,750 max x diam 240)
FINISH Steel / Glass shade
WATTAGE 60W max

- Ceiling cup contains an adjustable wire so the light can be high for overall illumination, and lower for task lighting over working areas. Shade is blown by mouth so each is unique.

DIMENSIONS H63 x diam 12
(H1,600 x diam 305)
FINISH Lacquered aluminum
WATTAGE 60W max

- This light can be hung from a ceiling hook. The light is focused downward, making it ideal for dining areas.

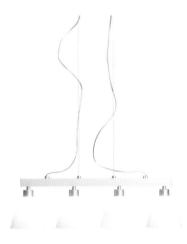

DIMENSIONS H69 max x diam 17³/₄
(H1,750 max x diam 450)
FINISH Lacquered aluminum
WATTAGE 60W max

● The ceiling cup in this model contains the
adjustable hanging mechanism so the
height can be adjusted through the handle.

DIMENSIONS H48³/₄ max x L22³/₄
(H1,240 max x L580)
FINISH Lacquered steel / Glass shade
WATTAGE 40W max each bulb

● The hanging wires can be adjusted for light
at the desired height. The four shades are
made from frosted glass so there is no glare.

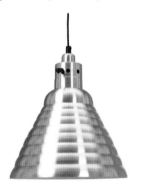

DIMENSIONS H72³/₄ x diam 12¹/₂
(H1,850 x diam 320)
FINISH Lacquered aluminum
WATTAGE 60W max

● This model can be hung from a ceiling hook
and is not adjustable. The shade focuses light
downward, making it ideal for use over
dining areas.

DIMENSIONS H68 x diam 14
(H1,730 x diam 360)
FINISH Painted aluminum
WATTAGE 60W max

● Featuring an S-shaped hook to adjust the
height without shortening the length of the
hanging wire, this is a good general light.

lighting / spotlights

DIMENSIONS H8 x diam 12
(H240 x diam 300)
FINISH Aluminum
WATTAGE 20W max each bulb

● **RIGHT** With three adjustable spotlights on
an aluminum track, this must be used with
reflector bulbs only. It gives a good level of
general illumination. Spotlights can be
angled in any direction.

DIMENSIONS L23¹/₂ (L600)
FINISH Lacquered steel
WATTAGE 20W max each bulb

● **LEFT** This model has four adjustable lamps,
for maximum flexibility. It must be sited at
least 12in (300mm) away from other objects,
as the halogen bulbs get very hot.

DIMENSIONS H10 x diam 9
(H250 x diam 230)
FINISH Chrome-plated steel / Glass
WATTAGE 35W max each bulb

● **RIGHT** This triple ceiling spotlight is
protected against water and moisture, so
could also be used in a bathroom.

DIMENSIONS H6³/₄ x diam 10¹/₄
(H170 x diam 260)
FINISH Nickel-plated steel
WATTAGE 35W max each bulb

● **LEFT** Four adjustable spotlights for
● maximum directional flexibility feature in
this steel model. The shade diameter of each
spotlight is 23/4in (70mm).

DIMENSIONS H10 x diam 13¹/₄
(H250 x diam 340)
FINISH Lacquered birch / Glass
WATTAGE 35W max each bulb

● **RIGHT** A triple adjustable spotlight, this can
● be screwed directly to the ceiling. Spotlights
can be moved to focus on walls, ceiling, or
floor for maximum flexibility.

DIMENSIONS H6³/₄ x diam 11³/₄
(H170 x diam 300)
FINISH Lacquered steel
WATTAGE 60W max each bulb

● **LEFT** With three adjustable spotlights, this
● model, finished in white, gives a good level
of general illumination.

DIMENSIONS H11³/₄ x L12¹/₄
(H300 x L310)
FINISH Lacquered steel / Chrome
WATTAGE 50W max

● **RIGHT** This single spotlight projects different
patterns and colors. It is adjustable, so can be
projected onto walls, floors, or ceiling.

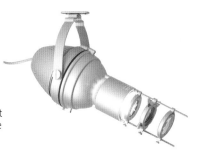

lighting / spotlights

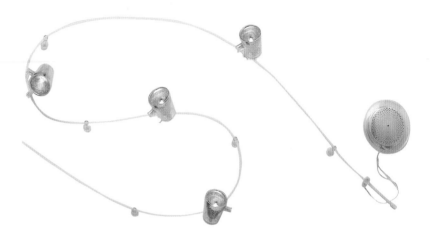

DIMENSIONS L 137³/₄ (L3,500)
FINISH Plastic
WATTAGE 20W max each bulb

● **ABOVE** Flexible, bendable lighting track with
five adjustable directional spotlights. The
track can be mounted to the ceiling or wall,
but must be sited 8in (200mm) from other
objects as the bulbs get hot.

DIMENSIONS Shade diam 6 (150)
FINISH Lacquered aluminum
WATTAGE 20W each bulb

● **BELOW** This model can be fitted with a
maximum of seven movable, adjustable
spotlights. It must be placed at least 12in
(300mm) from other objects, as halogen
spotlights get very hot.

DIMENSIONS H7½ x L35½ (H190 x L900)
FINISH Chrome-plated steel
WATTAGE 20W max each bulb

● **ABOVE** This model has four movable and
adjustable spotlights, each of which takes a
halogen bulb. It must be sited at least 16in
(400mm) from other objects, as the bulbs
get very hot.

DIMENSIONS H8¾ x L52¼ (H220 x L1,330)
FINISH Nickel-plated steel / Glass
WATTAGE 35W max each bulb

● **BELOW** With five adjustable spotlights, this
model also has two adjustable arms making
it easy to direct the lights exactly where
needed. It can be hung from a ceiling hook
or fixed with screws.

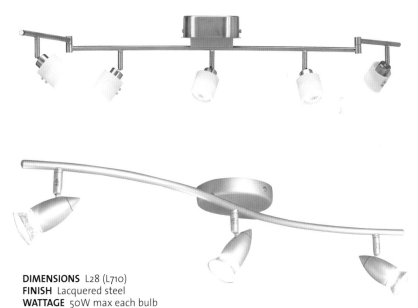

DIMENSIONS L28 (L710)
FINISH Lacquered steel
WATTAGE 50W max each bulb

● Adjustable three-bulb track light for good
general illumination. Takes three halogen
bulbs. Also available as a five-spot lodel.

lighting / spotlights

DIMENSIONS H3 max x diam 5
(H80 max x diam 130)
FINISH Bronze / Polished brass
WATTAGE 50W max

● A spotlight also available as a tilting model
● that can be used when tilted to highlight
wall features, or when untilted to contribute
to overall light levels. Also available with a
polished brass finish.

DIMENSIONS H$^3/_4$ x diam 4
(H20 x diam 100)
FINISH Antique brass
WATTAGE 50W max

● Fixed recessed down light, suitable for more
● traditional kitchens. Should be spaced at least
3ft (1m) from each other. Uses halogen bulbs.

DIMENSIONS H6 x diam 9$^1/_2$
(H150 x diam 240)
FINISH Antique brass
WATTAGE 50W max each bulb

● A three-light spotlight plate, this is suitable
● for ceilings only and is most effective used to
highlight wall features. The plate is spun
brass and the heads cast brass. The model
uses halogen bulbs.

chapter five

This chapter works in several different ways. At its start are split pages of kitchens in various different styles and colorways. These pages are split into four sections so that you can instantly see the effect of teaming wall cupboards, tiles and countertops, base cupboards, and floors in different finishes and materials. Turn these pages until you get a feel for what you might like in your kitchen. You may love an entire roomset, but you are more likely to mix and match from several of the photographs. The second part of the chapter picks up on the heart of the book, with a series of wish lists so that you make detailed notes of what you want to source and buy, when work begins in earnest. Finally, there are pages of grids and templates to allow you to get down to detailed planning.

wall cupboards

Ideas for wall cupboards feature at the top of each page. The pages show a range of different materials, finishes, and styles, both solid and glazed, for you to choose from.

tiles and countertop

The second section of the cut pages shows ideas for wall coverings, including tiles in different styles and colors, as well as splash boards, faucets, and countertops in a variety of finishes.

base cabinets and oven

Base units in a variety of styles and finishes form the third part of the cut pages. These feature a mix of freestanding and built-in models. This selection also includes an oven, the most common under-counter appliance.

flooring

At the bottom of each of the cut pages are ideas for floors. These are in a range of finishes, including tile in various colors and styles; wood in several different shades; vinyls; and linoleums.

wish lists

As you make decisions on appliances, cabinets, and accessories and gadgets, as well as all of the other items you wish to include in your kitchen, use these lists to keep a record of what you intend to buy. For ease of use, these pages can be removed so you can take them to the store or to your kitchen designer and installer with you. Note down model numbers and dimensions so you can be sure you buy exactly what you have decided upon. You can also use them to keep a record of costs, as well as to help you figure out the most appropriate supplier. They also allow you to see at a glance how the budget is shaping up. If you buy the bigger items first, this gives you the opportunity to add the finishing touches at a later date, if work goes over budget. These pages are also ideal to have on hand if you are sitting at your computer, ordering all of your appliances and equipment via the Internet. It is a good idea to start off your lists in pencil, as your initial thoughts are likely to change as you refine your search for essentials and desirables. It's worth photocopying a list before you erase any item, just in case you change your mind at a later date. File lists you no longer need in the ziplock pocket initially; later you may want to add them to your kitchen record book as a reminder of this project.

electrical appliances

item / supplier	color	cost
1		
2		
3		
4		
5		
6		
7		
8		
9		
10		
11		
12		

electrical appliances

item / supplier	color	cost
1		
2		
3		
4		
5		
6		
7		
8		
9		
10		
11		
12		

cabinet styles

item / supplier	color	cost
1		
2		
3		
4		
5		
6		
7		
8		
9		
10		
11		
12		

cabinet styles

item / supplier	color	cost
1		
2		
3		
4		
5		
6		
7		
8		
9		
10		
11		
12		

sink and faucets

item / supplier	color	cost
1		
2		
3		
4		
5		
6		
7		
8		
9		
10		
11		
12		

countertop and tiles

item / supplier	color	cost
1		
2		
3		
4		
5		
6		
7		
8		
9		
10		
11		
12		

countertop and tiles

item / supplier	color	cost
1		
2		
3		
4		
5		
6		
7		
8		
9		
10		
11		
12		

flooring materials

item / supplier	color	cost
1		
2		
3		
4		
5		
6		
7		
8		
9		
10		
11		
12		

flooring materials

item / supplier	color	cost
1		
2		
3		
4		
5		
6		
7		
8		
9		
10		
11		
12		

lighting fixtures

item / supplier	color	cost
1		
2		
3		
4		
5		
6		
7		
8		
9		
10		
11		
12		

lighting fixtures

item / supplier	color	cost
1		
2		
3		
4		
5		
6		
7		
8		
9		
10		
11		
12		

grids and templates

This last section of the mix-and-match chapter features grids and templates. The grids represent the floorplan of your kitchen. Before you can use them, it is important to take accurate measurements of all the dimensions of your kitchen. This should be done front to back and side to side. Take more than one measurement of each dimension since, in older properties in particular, most walls are not "square." It is not difficult to work around this, but you need to know where any anomalies lie. Measure, too, any structural elements you are going to keep, such as a chimney, as you will need to include this on your floorplan. The darker horizontal and vertical rules on the grids for the floorplan divide the plan into 12in., or 1ft, squares (30 cm squares). These are further divided by the paler rules into 3in. (750mm) squares. Select the grid that is most appropriate for your room. Taken together, the grids allow for a floorplan measuring 24ft x 31ft (7.3m x 9.5m). The templates represent the kitchen essentials you will be working with—appliances, sinks, stove tops, and ventilator hoods, as well as wall and base cabinets in several different dimensions. If you prefer to do your planning at a larger scale, or if your space is small or you are only remodeling part of the kitchen, then you could increase the sizes of both grids and templates using a photocopier. If you adopt this approach, be sure to increase everything by the same percentage so that the floorplans and templates remain in proportion.

organize your space / floorplans

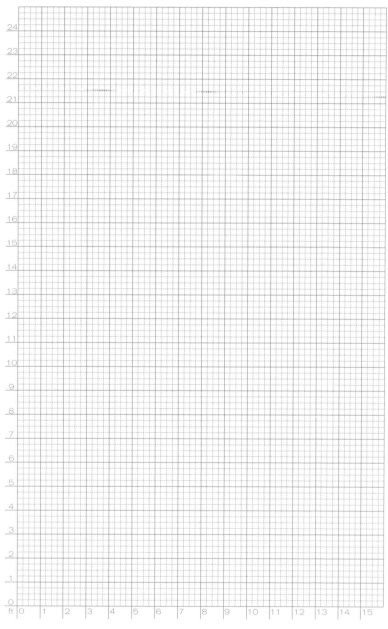

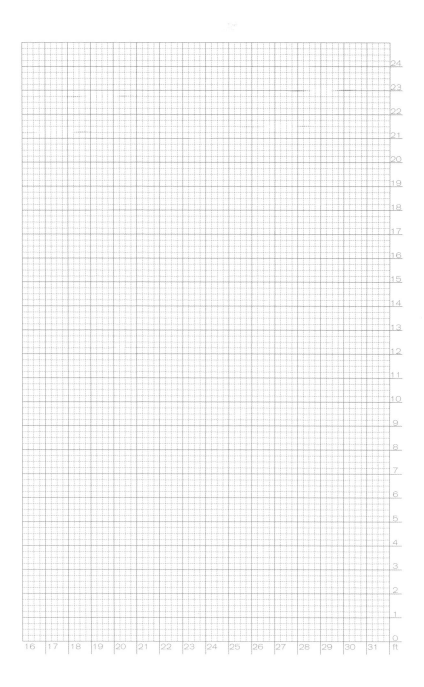

organize your space / templates

These templates represent the most common sizes of appliances and cabinets sold by off-the-shelf kitchen manufacturers. Either trace them off these pages, or photocopy the pages, and cut out the templates. You can then move these around on your floorplan to get an arrangement you like.

appliances

36in (900mm) appliance	36in (900mm) appliance	30in (750mm) appliance	24in (600mm) appliance	24in (600mm) appliance
36in (900mm) appliance	36in (900mm) appliance	30in (750mm) appliance	24in (600mm) appliance	24in (600mm) appliance
36in (900mm) appliance	36in (900mm) appliance	30in (750mm) appliance	24in (600mm) appliance	24in (600mm) appliance
36in (900mm) appliance	36in (900mm) appliance	30in (750mm) appliance	24in (600mm) appliance	24in (600mm) appliance

other considerations

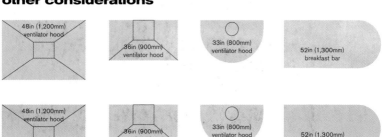

48in (1,200mm) ventilator hood

36in (900mm) ventilator hood

33in (800mm) ventilator hood

52in (1,300mm) breakfast bar

48in (1,200mm) ventilator hood

36in (900mm) ventilator hood

33in (800mm) ventilator hood

52in (1,300mm) breakfast bar

sink units

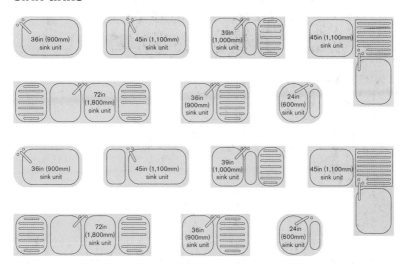

stove tops

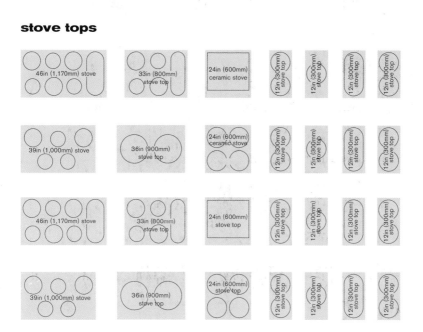

organize your space / templates

base and wall units

39in (1,000mm) base unit	36in (900mm) base unit	33in (800mm) base unit	24in (600mm) base unit	21in (500mm) base unit
39in (1,000mm) base unit	36in (900mm) base unit	33in (800mm) base unit	24in (600mm) base unit	21in (500mm) base unit
39in (1,000mm) base unit	36in (900mm) base unit	33in (800mm) base unit	24in (600mm) base unit	21in (500mm) base unit
39in (1,000mm) base unit	36in (900mm) base unit	33in (800mm) base unit	24in (600mm) base unit	21in (500mm) base unit

15in (400mm) base unit

12in (300mm) base unit

9in (200mm) base unit

24in (600mm) wall unit

21in (500mm) wall unit

24in (600mm) corner wall unit

12in (300mm) unit

12in (300mm) unit

24in (600mm) wall unit

21in (500mm) wall unit

12in (300mm) unit

15in (400mm) base unit

12in (300mm) base unit

9in (200mm) base unit

24in (600mm) wall unit

21in (500mm) wall unit

24in (600mm) corner wall unit

12in (300mm) unit

12in (300mm) unit

15in (400mm) base unit

12in (300mm) base unit

9in (200mm) base unit

15in (400mm) wall unit

12in (300mm) wall unit

9in (200mm)

24in (600mm) corner wall unit

12in (300mm) unit

12in (300mm) unit

15in (400mm) wall unit

12in (300mm) wall unit

9in (200mm)

12in (300mm) unit

15in (400mm) base unit

12in (300mm) base unit

9in (200mm) base unit

15in (400mm) wall unit

12in (300mm) wall unit

9in (200mm)

24in (600mm) corner wall unit

12in (300mm) unit

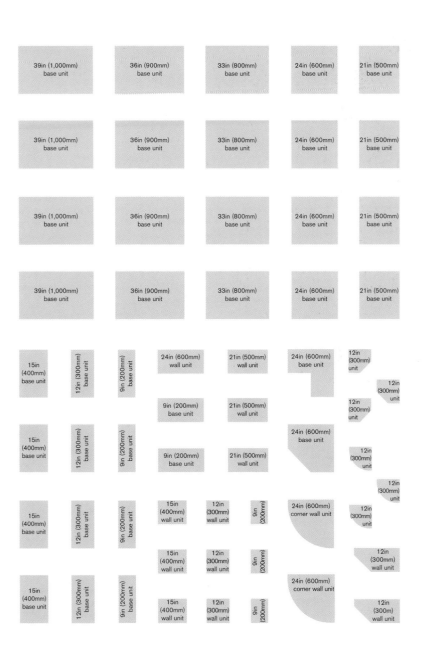

index / suppliers

The following companies produce all the kitchen products featured in the photographs in this book. Their website are the best place to start your search for products.

Aga
www.aga-ranges.com

Altima (Light Source)
www.lightsourceltd.co.uk

Amana
www.amana.com

American Woodmark
www.americanwoodmark.com

American Standard
www.americanstandard-us.com

Architerra
www.architerra.com

Avonite Surfaces
www.avonite.com

Biblos Lighting
www.bibloslighting.com

Blanco Sinks
www.blanco.co.uk

Brandon Cabinets
www.brandom.com

Buddy Rhodes
www.buddyrhodes.com

Bulthaup
www.bulthaup.com

CaesarStone Quartz Surfaces
www.caesarstoneus.com

Canyon Creek
www.canyoncreek.com

Caple Kitchens
00 44 870 6069606

CCS Stone Inc.
www.ccsstone.com

Chalon
www.chalon.com

Classic Brass
www.classic-brass.com

Cooper Lighting
www.cooperlighting.com

Crabtree Kitchens
www.crabtreekitchens.co.uk

Crown Point Cabinetry
www.crown-point.com

CVL Luminaires
www.e-cvl.com

index / suppliers

index / suppliers

index

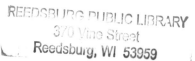

acknowledgements

Axis Publishing would like to thank the following companies for supplying images for inclusion in this book. If we have inadvertently failed to credit anyone, we will be happy to do so in any reprint.

Aga Ranges 5, 56, 57, 65b, 91, 99
Amana 54b, 58tl, tc, 61tl, bl, 62tl
American Standard 142, 143, 144, 145, 146, 147, 148, 149, 150, 151, 152, 153, 156, 157
Biblos Lighting 188, 189
Bulthaup 177
Canyon Creek 30, 33, 66b, 68–77, 78b, 80, 81b, 82–87, 89, 90t, 92–97. 100–19, 182b
Caple Kitchens 178b
Chalon 139t, 140t
Crabtree Kitchens 66t, 126, 127, 128, 130, 131, 132, 133, 134, 135, 136, 137, 138b, 168, 175t, 179b, 179, 180, 186b
Cullen Lighting 38, 39, 184, 185b, 186t
Enlightenment by Design/CVL Industries 190, 191t,b, 192, 193t
Enlightenment by Design/Limehouse Lighting 191r
Enlightenment by Design/Quality Lighting Design 193b, 200
Fisher & Paykel 44r, 45l, 48, 50t, 52, 53b, 54cb, 55cb, 59bl, 60br, 62b, 63b, 66t, c, 165, 173
General Electric 44l, 49b, 51, 65t, 66b
Green Mountain Soapstone 176
Hakatai/photography by Josh Perrin 32, 37b, 68–77, 82–77, 92–97, 100–19
Halo Art Glass 178t, 185t
Ikea 194–99
Jenn-air 1, 45r, 46l, 47r, 50b, 53t, 54ct, 55ct, b, 61br, 63t, br, 79, 120, 121b, 122t, 160, 161, 163t
Leisure Sinks 154, 155
Maytag 7, 54t, 55t, 58tr, 59br, 60t, bl
Plain & Fancy 78t, 127b, 138t, 140b, 159b, 166, 167, 169, 171
Shenandoah Cabinetry 68-77, 81t, 82–87, 88, 92–97, 100-119, 129, 139b, 141, 172b, 182t
Siematic 2/3, 10/11, 38/39, 65/66, 120/121, 122b, 172t, 175b, 200/201
Tanglewood Wine 162
Karen Verzariu 37t
Whirlpool 46r
Whitegood 163b, 174b, 187b

Illustrations on pp. 13, 15, 17, 19, 21, 23, 24, 25, 26. 27 by John Woodcock

Lorrie Mack is a freelance writer specializing in design and interiors. She is the author of over twelve books and is a regular contributor to newspapers and magazines.